REMEMBERING THE WAY IT WAS

Volume Two

REMEMBERING THE WAY IT WAS

Volume Two

More Stories from Hilton Head, Bluffton and Daufuskie

FRAN HEYWARD MARSCHER

Charleston · London

History
PRESS

Published by The History Press
Charleston, SC 29403
www.historypress.net

Cover art by Lynda K. Potter.

First published 2007

Manufactured in the United Kingdom

ISBN 978.1.59629.138.6

Library of Congress Cataloging-in-Publication Data

Marscher, Fran.
  Remembering the way it was, volume two: more stories from Hilton Head, Bluffton and Daufuskie/Fran Heyward Marscher.
     p. cm.
  ISBN 978-1-59629-138-6 (alk. paper)
  1. Oral history. 2. Hilton Head Island (S.C.)--Social life and customs--Anecdotes. 3. Bluffton (S.C.)--Social life and customs--Anecdotes. 4. Daufuskie Island (S.C.)--Social life and customs--Anecdotes. 5. Hilton Head Island (S.C.)--Biography--Anecdotes. 6. Bluffton (S.C.)--Biography--Anecdotes. 7. Daufuskie Island (S.C.)--Biography--Anecdotes. I. Title.
  F277.B3M25 2005
  975.7'99043'0922--dc22
  [B]

                          2005011679

Notice: The information in this book is true and complete to the best of our knowledge. It is offered without guarantee on the part of the author or The History Press. The author and The History Press disclaim all liability in connection with the use of this book.

CONTENTS

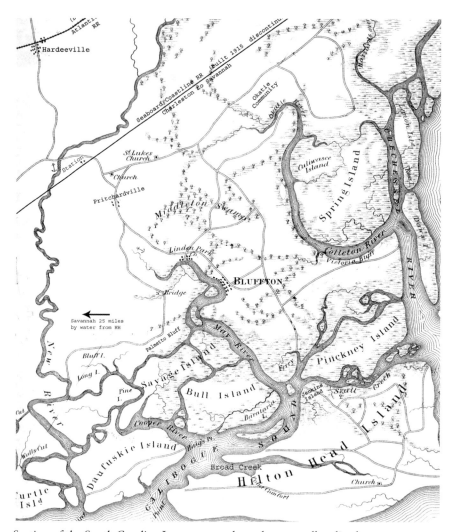

Section of the South Carolina Lowcountry where the storytellers lived.

INTRODUCTION

Like the Lowcountry players profiled in the first volume of this series, the characters here are as real as the live oaks that dominate the region. They grew up in the golden age of a golden place. With no gasoline engines, they had no traffic troubles. A fellow could ride his horse from Bluffton to the Buckingham Landing to catch a bateau to Hilton Head Island without seeing another person along the way. Without jet skis, he could travel silently through the creeks and sounds, relying on the tide and the wind to help power his oars or sails. He could hear the mullet jumping.

With no theaters or other forms of entertainment, the men and women in this book, calling on their imaginations to amuse themselves and amuse one another, became skilled storytellers. Crabs were so plentiful, they said, on a summer afternoon, even a child could walk along the creek's edge with one stout stick, throw dozens of them onto the bank, hook them with their back fins around a second stout stick and bring Mama enough crabs for supper. They told other stories: how Hilton Head Island became famous for butter beans, how Daufuskie built its reputation on its liquor stills and how the oyster-shell streets of Bluffton filled up with people three times a week when the important passenger and cargo steamers tied up to the dock at the end of Calhoun Street.

In 1900 all of Beaufort County had a population of only 35,000. By 1940, the population had dropped to 22,000, as blacks migrated to New York, Philadelphia, Detroit and Boston to look for wage-paying jobs nowhere to be found in South Carolina. By the 1960s, Beaufort County and Jasper County together were described as the heart of the nation's "poverty pocket."

Along came the beachfront resorts, the golf courses, tennis courts, retirement communities—and with them, dollars whipping through the local economy. Now, after half a century of developers marketing the area internationally the trappings of population growth have replaced much of the natural landscape. Everything is, as the Gullahs might say, "all change up."

And yet it still is possible from certain vantages to watch the tide slosh in and out twice a day, still possible to hear the squawk of blue herons and the rattle of wind in the palmettos. And it still is possible to go back to a slower and quieter era through the memories of the men and women in this book.

I interviewed most of these characters in the early 1980s when I was a reporter for the *Island Packet*, Hilton Head Island's daily newspaper. Most of the photographs are courtesy of the *Island Packet*. Others are courtesy of the subjects themselves, of family members or friends. My husband, Bill Marscher, who prodded me to polish these old tales and make them accessible for current and future generations, helped immensely in the process, especially with the pictures.

Perspective on Birth Years 1891–1900

Among those of us who live or vacation in the Lowcountry in the twenty-first century, there must be a special place in the heart for those who lived here more than a century ago.

They bonded with the region when the only relief from the press of a steamy August afternoon was a dip in the creek. They ran the place when water for drinking, cooking and washing had to be pumped by hand from a well in the yard, when toilets were mostly outdoor and mostly wooden. They had no paved roads and no need for any because they transported themselves, their families and their goods by foot or horse, by bateau or sailboat—except that one could catch the steamer for certain occasions.

Among most of the storytellers born here in the late 1800s, the theme of their lives was scratching out a living. Using their brawn and their brains, they wrenched turnips and a few rows of cotton out of the sandy soil; gathered musk, trapped coons and harvested pine resin from the virgin forests; harvested fish, shrimp, oysters and crabs from the tidal creeks.

"I've Done My Part"

As a young woman, Florence Duncan Jones Graham, born in 1892, lost two babies in the eighth month of pregnancy—so hardworking she had been, planting watermelon seeds in the cotton patch of Hilton Head Island's Spanish Wells community. She then outlived two husbands and two grown sons. Interviewed at the age of eighty-nine, Florence took a deep breath, rubbed her chest and recalled how lustily she once sang in the Mount Calvary Baptist

Church choir. For the interviewer that day, she sang softly, "Calvary, Calvary, where Jesus shed his blood for me. Calvary, Calvary, that's where my Savior died for me." Then, "I'm old now. No need for me to strain my weak lungs. Let the younger do the singing in church. I've done my part. I've got to take it easy."

Like most others of her time and place, Florence had never been a take-it-easy person. In her ninetieth year, she still puttered in her garden to make sure she had enough collard greens for the winter, still cleaned up leaves and tree limbs from around her house, still sang from time to time while she worked. She held her head high, proud of her intelligence, her agility and heritage.

What a huge mistake, though, to assume that every life in that time and place revolved around the grubby labor of constantly wrestling with Nature to put food on the table.

PASTRY CHEF AND MIDWIFE

When Mary Hamilton Jones was born in 1897 on Palmetto Bluff, several working plantations on the property there were all heavily planted and owned by R.T. Wilson, a wealthy New Yorker. Mary's mother and father worked on one plantation's cotton gin. As a child, Mary would carry lunch to her working parents—biscuits, sweet potatoes and maybe a bit of bacon.

As a teenager, Mary began to baby-sit children who would come with their parents to hunt on Palmetto Bluff. In 1917 one of the visiting women begged Mary to go back to New York with her family to continue working as the children's "nurse." So, at the age of twenty, Mary took what she called "a lovely train trip" and spent that summer in the big city.

A couple of years later, Mary married young Benjamin Jones of Hilton Head Island, a man who gave up oyster picking to become a fishing guide and chef for the wealthy Palmetto Bluff owners and guests. In 1919 Mary and Benjamin took a glamorous honeymoon trip—the adventure of a young Southern black couple's lifetime—from Savannah to New York City on a cruise ship. For the next year, they worked as cooks for the Wilsons in New York, enjoying the bright lights and other amenities of the metropolis. They then settled down in Hilton Head's Jonesville, a tract of land between Jarvis Creek and Old House Creek, where they raised four children, including the youngest, David "Come See" Jones, profiled in part two of this volume.

During the winters, Mary and Benjamin Jones cooked for Honey Horn Plantation, owned in the early part of the century by W.P. Clyde, then by Roy Rainey, and in the 1930s and 1940s by Landon Thorne and Alfred Loomis. Mary remembered the kitchen there as a warm, sweet-smelling place with a wood-burning stove so big it took two women to open the oven door. The Jones couple specialized in pastry and made their own mayonnaise. The diners would number seven to ten daily—the owners, a few friends, a butler and a maid. After Benjamin died, Mary continued cooking for a living for another ten years. After leaving Honey Horn, she worked in the restaurant of William Hilton Inn, the island's first resort, until she retired.

In the 1960s, when Mary was in her sixties, she took a ten-day class in midwifery from an African woman at Penn Center, and the State Department of Health and Environmental Control licensed her to practice. At the time, there was neither an obstetrician nor a hospital in southern Beaufort County. There was one physician in Bluffton, but he had no labor ward, no delivery room, no nursery and no incubators. There was a bridge from Hilton Head to the mainland, but there was no rescue squad. Hilton Head Island needed a midwife.

Most of the babies Mary "caught," she said, were healthy and beautiful, and most of the mothers needed only tender, loving care. The care-giving was what Mary enjoyed most. The skills of delivery Mary learned from an expert, but the care she gave to the women developed out of years of living and learning the value of looking after one another. "A lot of what I was able to do came," she said, "from what my people gave me."

Like Florence Graham and Mary Jones, the other characters of this southernmost corner of coastal South Carolina spoke in the 1980s with pride and joy rather than with despair about their strategies for keeping body and soul together. They had to be resourceful. They designed and built their rowboats and sailboats to meet their needs in the region's vast and varied estuarine system. Out of cotton twine they knitted cast nets for seafood, wide mesh for mullet, narrow mesh for shrimp. They created beautiful coiled baskets for utilitarian purposes out of sweet grass, pine needles and palmetto fronds. They smoked and salted pork and gathered, dried and steeped the roots, twigs and leaves of wild plants to relieve various maladies. They made blackberry wine, made music, made quilts out of scrap fabric. They prayed and praised God.

In 1891 an earthquake in Japan killed as many as ten thousand people. In 1892 Tchaikovsky's *The Nutcracker* ballet opened in St. Petersburg, Russia. In 1893 Henry Ford built his first car. In 1894 Rudyard Kipling published *The Jungle Book*. In 1895 Cuba fought Spain for its independence. In 1896 Utah became a state. In 1897 Rodin completed the Victor Hugo sculpture. In 1898 the first photographs using artificial light were taken. In 1899 sound was recorded for the first time magnetically. In 1900 Renoir painted *Nude in the Sun*.

Except for the hurricane that drowned as many as two thousand residents of South Carolina's islands and lowlands in 1893, nothing much of national or international significance happened in the Lowcountry in those years. The okra grew tall, and quail were plentiful in the fields.

Floriner Bush Duggans and Katie Bush Mangum.

A Pleasant Life on Meager Resources

Katie Bush Mangum
Born in 1891

Floriner Bush Duggans
Born circa 1900

You have to skin the 'coon and cut the musk [scent glands] *out of the hind legs. You cut off the head and parboil it. Then you put some salt and pepper and onion on it and shove it in the oven. Let it cook slow, and you've got something good.*

As a little girl growing up in the Okatie, near the present Sun City Hilton Head, Katie Bush Mangum played with two kinds of dolls.

When she was ninety, she challenged me, "Do you know how to make dolls out of grass?"

Then she gave away her secret method: "I'd pull a bunch of grass up out of the ground and take a comb and comb out all the little roots. The roots would be the doll's hair. Then I'd wrap a little rag around the blades of grass for the body. I'd pull out some of the grass on the sides for arms and make a little sleeve. Sometimes I'd give it a hat out of a scrap."

Then one Christmas, in a stocking hung by the chimney with care, Santa Claus left a piece of candy, an apple and a little iron doll. "I was proudest of that," she said.

Born in 1891, the oldest of fourteen children of George and Molly Jones Bush, Katie was reared by her grandfather and a step-grandmother on a small cotton farm near Pepper Hall Plantation in southern Beaufort County. She played in a dirt yard and fished and crabbed in "the crick" (the creek), "Melon Hole" in the Okatie River. The game of "Shoo, Turkey, Shoo" didn't cost any money, but it brought a lot of giggling. Katie remembered the words "fly to the east, fly to the west" but not much more about it. It involved holding hands, forming a circle and "having fun."

Katie's grandfather, Papa, a quiet, religious man, would use the expletive "Confound!" occasionally, but otherwise never exhibited anger or ill temper. In addition to his cotton to produce cash once a year, he planted peas, corn and potatoes for the table. He took his family on Sundays to the St. Matthew Baptist Church.

The Okatie children's formal education occurred in the months of December, January and February only. Occasionally they would walk or ride the horse and buggy to Bluffton to shop or catch a steamer to Savannah.

When Katie was thirteen, she caught double pneumonia, stiffened up and was marked for death by the community's health experts. There were no emergency rooms, no doctors, no hospitals. There was no antibiotic. There was not even an aspirin. Pulling through that bout of illness was a source of pride to her three quarters of a century later. "They said I wouldn't live, but I'm here yet," she said, chortling.

'COON AND 'POSSUM AND CHARLESTON

While Katie was growing up with her grandparents on the Okatie, her half-sister Floriner, who was a few years younger, was growing up with her parents in the nearby Bull Hill section of the Okatie. Floriner's father made a living at a trade Floriner called "chip box" and "dip gum." It was the business of tapping the region's fragrant pine trees and selling their sticky sap for resin and turpentine, taking it for distillation to a still in Pritchardville.

Drawing on her memory of childhood at Bull Hill, Floriner gave me instructions for preparing raccoon and opossum for the table: "You have to skin the 'coon and cut the musk [scent glands] out of the hind legs. You cut off the head and parboil it. Then you put some salt and pepper and onion on it and shove it in the oven. Let it cook slow, and you've got something good. Now a 'possum. That's fine. When a 'possum's fat, he's better than 'coon. You cook them the same way."

At the age of six, Floriner began working for the white Verdier family, helping in the house, taking care of the Verdier children. When the Verdiers moved to Charleston, she moved with them. When she was older, she married a man in the "chip box" and "dip gum" trade, same as her father. He later drove a delivery truck in Charleston, where Floriner lived for about forty-five years before moving back home to the Okatie.

When she was eighteen or nineteen, when a bag full of groceries cost only about twenty-five cents, she moved to Savannah to live with an aunt and to take a job washing dishes for one dollar per week. In 1912 she married a longshoreman, had a miscarriage soon afterward as a result of her only pregnancy and then separated from her husband. Like many other blacks in those years, Katie lived up North for a while before returning home. In 1915 she moved to New York City to look for work as a housekeeper.

In New York, hired as a housekeeper and a cook, Katie had to get a book to learn to cook mashed potatoes instead of the familiar grits and rice on which she had been brought up. But she figured it out. She managed in the strange, big city, she said, because she could "mostly get along with anybody" and had no trouble keeping a job. The Statue of Liberty and the subways made a lasting impression on her. "I took excursions out to see things. I had a half-sister, Elizabeth, living in the Bronx that I would go on the subway to visit. People were nice. They'd help you," she said.

"The best part, though, was the church. We'd spend all day Sunday at the church, having the gospel chorus and the breakfasts and the dinners. I was on the mission board. We held meetings and took up collections for the destitute. We'd take them food or money and pray for them. There was always some enjoyment in the church in New York."

In New York, Katie married twice, both times to longshoremen, and raised a niece.

KATIE AND FLORINER BACK HOME

Decades later, when their mother's health began to fail and their sisters asked for help to care for her, both Katie and Floriner returned to their family's home at Bull Hill. The two sisters made two apartments in their mother's old home and eventually took in a half-sister on Katie's father's side, no relation to Floriner.

In 1981, at the age of ninety, Katie Mangum shared a small frame house without running water with two half-sisters, unrelated to one another, ages eighty-four and eighty-one. When their Social Security checks came in at the first of every month, a nearby "niece-in-law" took Floriner shopping for them all. Floriner was still cooking on a wood-burning stove, proud that smoke out of the stovepipe signaled to her neighbors when she was baking.

Despite their years of experience that likely made them wise, except for the instructions on cooking 'coon and 'possum and making a child's toy doll out of grass, neither Katie nor Floriner gave advice to others. Pressed for a few words of wisdom, Katie slowly remembered a few themes from her Bush family traditions:

"Take care and use the least you can. Throw some back for a rainy day. Also, govern your passion. If you speak to people rash, you can cause tension. Be nice and you'll get it back."

Rosa Chisolm.

Meals out of the Creek

Rosa Chisolm
Born in 1896

At home in the water as well as on land, they often sailed to Bluffton to buy the things they could not raise or catch or make for themselves.

At the age of eighty-five, living alone in a mobile home in the Spanish Wells area of Hilton Head Island, Rosa Williams Chisolm could remember how it was when she was a child. Her father "could always catch crab and get conch" when other meat was scarce for his family of six. Rosa said she loved both. She often thought about how it was when her husband fished for a living. Seafood was the family's staple. Rosa would roll her big brown eyes. "Fish and sweet taters. That's what I loved," she said.

Born on Braddock's Point in what is now Sea Pines in about 1896, Rosa grew up in a thriving community there. Although the deer "always cleaned out the peas," she said, her father, Julius Williams, grew enough corn, beans, sugar cane and okra for the table while raising cotton for cash.

In the good years, Rosa and the other neighborhood children—called the "Point Children"—went to school from November to March. She explained that it wasn't possible in those days to have a school all the time but that the men would get together after a season of good crops and "work up a school for us." Many children didn't begin their formal education at all until the age of ten or eleven. "We were big children before we started lessons," she said. "That's why we learned so good."

When the Point Children weren't doing their lessons in the early 1900s, they hoed and picked in the fields of Henry Padgett, a white man. They went swimming in the same creek that produced the fish for supper. After fourth grade, Rosa decided she liked the work in the fields so much and could make so much money that she dropped out of school. Mr. Padgett, she said, found her to be such a good farm worker that he paid her as much as he paid her mother.

Buggy Rides to Church

There was no church on Braddock's Point. For the families who lived there, getting to services at the old Oak Grove Church on what is now Mathews Drive was a weekend production. Once a quarter, the Point families would travel by horse and buggy and on foot to spend Saturday night with relatives or friends somewhere in the middle of the island. "All the roads would be crowded up with people," Rosa said as she recalled those days. They would go to church Sunday morning and walk or ride in a buggy back to Braddock's Point on Sunday afternoon.

Since there was only a small store on the south end of the island, Renty Miller's store at Point Comfort, the Point families sometimes traveled to the north end to shop. At home in the water as well as on land, they often sailed to Bluffton instead to buy the things they could not raise or catch or make for themselves. To the young girl who spent so much time working in the gray sandy soil, the colorful patterns on the bolts of cloth in Bluffton stores were the prettiest things she had ever seen.

In 1913 Rosa married Reuben Chisolm, a young man also born on Hilton Head to a family of fishermen and farmers. Reuben and Rosa settled in the old Lawton Plantation on a spot near the present Heritage Farm. Like their parents, the couple grew some cotton. He fished Calibogue Sound, Broad Creek and Lawton Creek. Reuben used hooks and lines, cast nets and gill nets to catch croaker, whiting, trout, flounder, crabs, shrimp and anything else he could get out of the water to sell. "He had been raised up in the creek," Rosa said. "If it was in there, he could catch it. We ate so much fish then, sometimes I wished I had married a butcher so I could get some meat," she said, laughing.

Reuben Chisolm stored his catch all week long in ice he "hired," in Rosa's words, from the "line boat" that traveled between Savannah and Beaufort. On Thursdays or Fridays he hauled it from Lawton Landing to Savannah by sailboat, taking advantage of the tide as well as the wind as much as possible.

Rosa sailed with him to Savannah sometimes, glad to have a chance to see the sights and buy a few things there, but wary of what she called "big water" between Hilton Head Island and Savannah. "I didn't mind it when it was little waves," she said, motioning with her hands. "But when it was rough, oh boy! Sometimes the gunwale would almost go underwater. I'd climb to the other side. My heart would almost come out of my body, I was so scared."

Honey Horn Plantation and the southern tip of Hilton Head Island, including Lawton Plantation, changed hands after the stock market crash of 1929, ending the era in which tenants paid no rent for living on the land. The new owners, Landon Thorne and Alfred Loomis, cleared their property of residents. Reuben and Rosa Chisolm then bought two acres in Spanish Wells, just across Broad Creek, and Reuben kept on fishing.

From time to time, Reuben would go off to Savannah to find jobs. He would bring beef back when he came on weekends. Rosa, Reuben and their children also gathered and sold musk, a native Lowcountry plant once used widely for its fragrance. As Rosa remembered it, during World War II, musk was "worth plenty" at the processing barn in Bluffton, and they "could gather plenty of it."

Hand "Good for the Crops"

In those years, Rosa was occupied bearing children, tending to babies and having miscarriages. She got pregnant sixteen times in the thirty-three years she was married. In addition to raising youngsters, she raised "more than a garden," she said. "I farmed. I made plenty of beans and everything. One year I made a truck full of cotton—me and my children. I didn't mind doing it either. I liked opening up the row and putting the corn in. My hand was good for the crops."

When Rosa was seventy-five, she was hoeing a row one spring and caught herself turning around to see how far she'd come, then looking forward to see how much farther she had to go. "When that happened, I said, 'Lord, just let me finish this garden, and I'll never put my hand to a hoe no more.' And that was the last year I planted.

"But I've done my share of work. I satify [sic]," she said.

In her later years, Rosa enjoyed a few adventures that took her away from the familiar soil. She traveled to Boston by bus three times, staying three months once and sightseeing with her children and grandchildren. She liked Boston. She had cataract surgery in the Hilton Head Hospital, and she liked the hospital staff and the results of her operation.

"A soon as I could see again [after the operation], I could cook for myself. I put on a pot of beans with pigs' feet, and it was so good," she said.

In her eighth decade, Rosa's pleasures included a pipe of tobacco and a can of Pabst Blue Ribbon every evening while she watched the news on TV—as well as her memories. She often thought back to big cotton crops, buggy rides to church, flounder catches, spring tides, sailboat rides to Savannah and meals of soul food, especially seafood.

"Fish and sweet potatoes," she said, smiling. "And a little grits. When I was in Boston I knew something was missing, but I couldn't figure it out. It was grits. I have to have my grits—and a little bit of fish."

Nellie Johnson White.

CROPS AND LESSONS

Nellie Johnson White
Born in 1896

She learned quickly that those with reading, writing and arithmetic skills
earned more and had a better life than those who depended on strong hands
and strong backs to make a living.

Nellie Johnson White, Ben White's third wife, was stepmother of eight children, mother of seven. The fifteen youngsters in her household spent their childhoods plowing, planting and harvesting—and going to school, studying by kerosene lanterns and doing homework. At the age of eighty-seven, Nellie was proud of her and Ben's offspring.

Although Nellie's own education—mostly in the small Chaplin Plantation School for blacks—had ended early, in the 1980s her family reunions drew together a host of schoolteachers and school principals from all over the country. Of Nellie's seven children, all but one graduated from college and several earned doctorate degrees. The several dozen grandchildren came along in the same footsteps, many educators among them.

Nellie was born at Folly Field in 1896, the daughter of a farmer and carpenter who took his produce to the Savannah markets by a sailboat. As a young girl, Nellie shucked oysters in L.P. Maggioni and Company's factory on Jenkins Island for only a couple of weeks before realizing that factory work was not for her. She moved to Savannah to live with cousins and work in laundries and restaurants. There she learned quickly that those skilled in reading, writing and arithmetic earned more and had a better life than those who depended on strong hands and strong backs to make a living.

Ben White was a widower, born on Hilton Head in 1886; he had been married twice and had fathered eight children before he and Nellie were married. What Nellie had learned by working in Savannah reinforced Ben White's family tradition of pushing education as a way out of poverty and problems. Nellie and Ben believed in discipline. Nellie said they would tell the children what they could do and what they could not do, and they expected obedience. When the children disobeyed, "They'd apologize," she said.

Habits of Effective People

"I always wanted my children to grow up to have more learning than I did," Nellie said. Even for a reasonably prosperous farmer, the expense of private education and college education—at the Penn and Mather Schools in the Beaufort area as well as at Savannah State, South Carolina State and other colleges—was daunting, but Ben and Nellie believed in sacrifice for the children they loved. "We afforded the schooling for the children," Nellie explained, "by getting only what we had to have, not necessarily all that we wanted."

For many years, for that huge family, Nellie cooked on a wood-burning stove, washed clothes with a scrub board and an outdoor wash pot, drew water from an outdoor well. All the while, she said over and over to her children, "Get yourself educated."

By the 1980s, Nellie was living in a big, brick house with fine indoor plumbing and electricity and modern appliances. She gave credit for her comfort to the sons and daughters she and Ben had reared.

"If you take care of children, they'll help you later," she said. "I wouldn't have any income but for them. They don't forget."

They didn't forget Nellie and didn't forget the vegetables raised by the ton on Hilton Head Island when they were growing up. For decades, the children kept coming back—with their own children and grandchildren—to renew the ties that bound them together. At their traditional family reunions, they dined on rice and peas and beans and okra and sweet potatoes and ham and fried chicken. By then, not only did they not have to raise all the food themselves, but they also hired caterers to do the shopping, the preparation and the serving for their family gatherings. At their reunions, they had a lot of catching up to do, a lot of talking about the way it was on Hilton Head Island long ago.

Nellie Johnson White was stepmother of Johnny White, who was profiled in the first volume of this series.

Sarah Kellerson Bradley.

Living Demanded Brawn and Brain

Sarah Kellerson Bradley
Born in 1896

She would fling a crab out of the water onto the bank,
then grab his back fins with her bare hands.

On the surface, Sarah Kellerson Bradley led a simple life. Sarah never had to deal with tight flight connections, malfunctioning software or the exchange of foreign currency. She was not into business or competitive sports or the arts. She spent no time trying to influence public policy. In the early 1980s, from the porch of the home she lived in with her granddaughter, she could point to the spot where she was "birthed" in 1896, "right under that tree," she said.

Although by many standards Sarah and her family lived simply, they did not live easily. "Making it" in Sarah's day required ingenuity and repetitive labor. In a lifetime on Hilton Head Island, Sarah learned the hard way to keep body and soul together through sheer physical prowess. She survived some tough times as a do-it-yourself person.

Sarah's ancestors on her mother's side—the Walters—fled to South Carolina from Darien, Georgia, during the Civil War. The Walters family planted cotton on Hilton Head, sending it by freight sailboat to the Waterhouse gin in Beaufort.

Sometime before the turn of the century, one of the Walters daughters, Venus, married an island boy, Edward Kellerson. Venus and Edward raised cotton, collard greens, sweet potatoes and watermelons and began raising three children before they "parted," according to Sarah, their middle child. Venus was left to take care of the offspring on her own when Edward moved to Savannah to work as a butcher.

Yanking a Living out of the Sandy Soil

Asked how young Venus, her mother, managed to feed, shelter and clothe a family on a remote barrier island, Sarah Kellerson Bradley explained with demonstrative hands. Her long fingers reaching out in front of her, her wrists flexing, her muscles taut, she made the motions of working in the fields.

Venus and her children hired themselves out to plant, hoe and harvest crops on other islanders' farms. Sarah said she had learned by the age of seven how to milk a cow and by the age of ten how to pick cotton. The family fed chickens and sold eggs for ten cents a dozen. They raised turkeys, beans and peas to sell in the Savannah City Market. Picking beans and peas was backbreaking work, but at least the beans and peas didn't bite. Sarah remembered many times as a child going to "see about" a turkey's nest and having the hen turkey peck her on the hand and flap her wings in a brazen scare tactic. But of all the work on the farm, "hoeing was the hardest," Sarah said, remembering the long rows of sandy black soil.

Unique Crabbing Method

Sarah's mother and her sisters developed the skills to go after everything edible in the surrounding waters. Sarah became proficient in snagging the wily Atlantic blue crabs just off the bluff of her family's property. She had no traps, no baskets, no string. Using only a stick for tackle, she did it this way: "The crab would be right at the edge of the water. I'd take a stick to push it out. If he buried himself, I'd have to dig up the mud to get him." She would fling a crab out of the creek onto the bank, then grab his back fins with her bare hands. If the crab was faster than she was, he might pinch her with his powerful claws, but Sarah said she would just jerk her hand back to save herself. One by one, Sarah strung the wriggling crabs onto the limb of a palmetto tree, hooking them on with their fins and claws.

By the age of eighty-five, Sarah guessed her arthritis might hamper her in crabbing. But she was proud of how she could do it.

"If you do it right with the palmetto limb, they couldn't get away," she said. "I didn't even need no bucket."

To catch trout and bass in the winter and whiting, blackfish, yellowtail and catfish in the summer, they dangled a sinker and a hook with a piece of shrimp on it tied to a hand line. Oysters lying on the creek banks were free for the picking up. Shrimp, schooling in the summer and early fall, were free for those skilled with the cast net. Gathering seafood for the table was as routine as planting watermelons. Sarah continued with it most of her life.

WATER AS DANGER

Sarah was only twelve years old when she took her last boat ride in about 1908: "I had rowed across the crick [Skull Creek] myself," she explained, using her arms to show how she handled the oars in the flat-bottomed bateau. "Just as I was about to come back, a big boat started coming down the crick, building up waves in the water," she said, gesturing to give me a feel for the size of the chop in the creek.

"I was so scared. I was afraid I couldn't get 'cross without turning over or gettin' run over by the boat. I didn't know if I'd ever get 'cross that channel again.

"But my mother was on the other side, and she motion to me, and I pick up my nerve and row it hard." She gave the rowing motion with her arms once more.

"I finally got 'cross, and I don't get in a boat again since then."

Sarah was afraid of the water because, despite living on an island for almost a century, she never learned to swim. No one ever suggested that she could. She remembered enjoying wading "just on the edge of the 'crick,'" but would never go out, she said, "where the feet couldn't touch." Although she had ready access for decades to the twelve miles of Hilton Head Island beach now in great demand, she could recall going to the beach only twice in her entire life. She said she had "no business" on the south end of the island either and did not remember ever going much beyond "Stoney" (near the present-day Islanders' Park).

As for her education, Sarah walked the dirt road to the school for blacks at Honey Horn. The term was three months per year. Sarah went to classes for three years, for a total of about nine months all together, before quitting school to work in the fields.

And Sarah's adult life copied her childhood—organized around the growing seasons and the tides. She and her second husband worked together in L.P. Maggioni's Jenkins Island oyster factory. To get to work, they walked eight to ten miles.

TO SEW A DRESS

For Sarah, cash was always scarce. She remembered that growing up she would have only one pair of shoes at a time, and her mother would insist that she "save them for church."

Rather than buy dresses for her own daughters, Sarah would choose cloth for ten cents a yard from among dozens of bolts of bright fabric in "Willie" Brown's store at the Crossroads (near the present-day Hilton Head Medical Center and Clinics). But she never bought dress patterns. She designed clothing in her head and then cut and sewed with her fingers.

For fun, Sarah, her cousins and friends danced to a homegrown band that played frequently in "Jonesville" (around Spanish Wells Road). On Christmas, groups of them would walk from house to house, eating, singing and drinking homemade wine.

Making the wine was one of Sarah's jobs. She would pack the wild blackberries or the wild grapes of summer in a jar, leave them six days and then squeeze them. "After six days, you t'row in some sugar," she said. Then she would pour the juice back into the jar and "let it work" for six more days. She would then strain the juice several times. Left to age over the fall, the wild blackberry or wild grape wine would taste "real good" by Christmas. Sarah licked her lips with pleasure as she remembered.

At the age of eighty-five, Sarah happily recalled another taste from the past. Islanders would rob the nests of loggerhead turtles, boil the eggs and suck them out. With each nest holding one hundred eggs or more, discovery of a nest in the sand dunes meant a lot of free protein as well as a feast for a crowd. "And they taste so good," Sarah said. A threatened species now, loggerheads, along with their eggs, are protected by federal law. It's likely that only a few folks living anywhere today have ever had the pleasure of eating them.

Sarah married twice and outlived both husbands—and also outlived all six of her children.

The conveniences that accompanied the modern development of Hilton Head Island made her happy. Pavement on the roads meant not having to get her feet muddy walking around the island in the rain. Electricity meant lights that could be switched on and that did not depend on kerosene. Running water in the house softened what had been the hard work for most of her life—cooking and washing.

By the 1980s, she was mighty happy not to have to hoe the soil to make food crops, joyous not to have to investigate the eggs in the nest of a setting turkey hen. Her happiness and joy was not only for her but also for her granddaughter and everybody else who lived on Hilton Head Island.

Catherine, Buster and Helen Martin. *Courtesy of Bud Martin.*

Northern Pride in the Lowcountry

Helen McCann Martin
Born in 1897

Her memories of Bluffton included "very good times, plenty of servants, lots of parties." They also included the sale in 1930 of a big chunk of Hilton Head Island, largely for its value as quail habitat.

Despite her mother's warning about malaria in South Carolina, in 1918 Helen McCann of Newark, New Jersey, married a South Carolinian—Clarence "Buster" Martin—a young man working temporarily in a New Jersey munitions factory. After the wedding, the newlyweds caught a train south, and after a brief stay in Savannah's DeSoto Hotel, boarded a steamer to Bluffton. "It was December—rainy and cool," Helen said. "The steamer would stop at the islands and people would row out to it to pick up groceries and make deliveries. They spoke Gullah everywhere, and I didn't understand what they were saying. Everybody came down to the boat when it got to Bluffton."

Wearing a red hat and white gloves, Helen made a unique fashion statement when she stepped off the boat. Helen and Buster had come for a six-week visit with Buster's family, the Martins, who lived in a big house on the bluff of the May River, across the "skid" (walking bridge) over Heyward Cove from the main part of town. Everything there was different from what she had known in New Jersey. Following the pattern of other Lowcountry houses at the time, the Martins' kitchen was a separate building. To Helen, this was a new arrangement. Buster's father had a turpentine business, and he "clubbed" (booking hunting parties) on Spring Island for a living. More than sixty years after Helen's first visit to Bluffton, she recalled "an old cedar tree" the Martins decorated for Christmas that year. It did not impress her.

Buster and Helen returned to New Jersey to live for a few more years and then moved back to southern Beaufort County. After all, Helen had not caught malaria on her first trip. In 1921, Buster started the Broad River Packing Company, a firm consisting of an oyster factory on Sawmill Creek and a seafood and vegetable packing business. He sold it in 1931.

Hilton Head's Quail

Helen's memories of Bluffton in the 1920s, 1930s and 1940s included "very good times, plenty of servants, lots of parties." She came to love the village and the river. Her memories also included the sale in 1930 of a big chunk of Hilton Head Island, largely for its value as quail habitat.

Roy Rainey, the flamboyant owner of Honey Horn Plantation and other Hilton Head property, had lost money big time in the stock market crash. Hoping for cash out of his land, he hired Allyne Martin, Helen's sister-in-law, as his broker. Allyne made Helen her chauffeur.

Alfred Loomis and Landon Thorne of New York, brothers-in-law and wealthy financiers who had cashed out before the market tanked, were looking for a getaway hunting preserve in the South. Helen helped them find it by picking them up at the Jasper County home of Marshall Field, owner of Chelsea Plantation, and driving them to Buckingham to catch a bateau ferry to Hilton Head. There they mounted waiting horses to explore the island for a quick bird survey.

"Allyne was so hoping that everything would go just perfect. She'd have died if they hadn't found any quail. But they did—several coveys. They decided to make the [property] purchase, so Allyne had a good day."

Further evidence of the huge bird population came in the fall of 1936 when, according to *Hilton Head: A Sea Island Chronicle* by Virginia Holmgren, Thorne and Loomis's gamekeeper flushed 293 coveys of quail. The gamekeeper also estimated the presence of 4,000 widgeons and reported that 18 to 20 other kinds of ducks were wintering on Hilton Head Island that year.

On the day of the big land sale, Helen had to drive her 1930 vintage automobile as fast as she could, probably at least thirty miles an hour, bouncing and swaying over sandy two-rutted roads to Ridgeland to the railroad station. She did manage to get Thorne and Loomis there in time to catch the train that afternoon.

A politician and public servant by nature, Helen's husband, Buster, served on the Beaufort County Commission from 1928 to 1931 and in the State Legislature from 1921 to 1934. Through U.S. Senator "Cottonhead" Smith, he got a job as division manager for the U.S. Department of Commerce, with headquarters in Charleston in 1934, so Buster and Helen moved to James Island.

Helen and Buster reared a son, Clarence, called "Bud," and a daughter, Catherine, bringing them back to Bluffton to spend summers throughout their childhood. Decades later, Helen recalled they felt it important to get the children out of congested Charleston because of the "polio scare." Another reason for spending summers in Bluffton was "because it was Buster's home and because he liked to fish in the May River."

Despite not being a native of Beaufort County, Helen McCann Martin cut a swath through Bluffton in the heyday of its earlier time as a small regional center of commerce for this corner of the rural Lowcountry.

Gerald Watkins with boats. *Courtesy of H.H. "Bubba" Von Harten.*

A Man and His Boats

Gerald Watkins
Born in 1898

I built seven big boats. They were good boats too. They didn't leak a drop of water. And when the bow went down in a heavy sea, she came back up. All the little ones I built were good for what I designed them for. And they didn't leak either.

Gerald Watkins bonded with the boats he built the way a mother bonds with a child. Details about the ribs and the beams, the bows, the planks and the decks of boats that he had given birth to decades earlier were fresh in his mind when I interviewed him in 1981. While watching a TV news clip about a marijuana bust off the Florida coast the year before, Gerald said he spotted a fifty-five-foot shrimp trawler he had designed and constructed in Key West in the early 1950s. Her name, *Sea Witch*, could have been attached to any boat, but Gerald didn't recognize the boat by her name but by the part of her that plowed headfirst through the water.

"I built that bow. I'll never forget her," he said.

Dozens of vessels for which Gerald drafted plans, hired carpenters and screwed in bolts in his younger days continued to serve their owners long after he retired.

Daufuskie, a fifty-five-footer weighing forty-eight tons and still shrimping for Wallace Wise in the 1980s, was one Gerald built in 1948. *Tugadoo*, Gilbert Maggioni's oyster barge, was another Gerald remembered well. He built *Captain Geech*, a sixty-one-foot trawler, for Herman Henry "Geech" Von Harten and *Miss Beaufort*, an identical boat, for another Beaufort-area shrimper. Also on Gerald's list was a forty-two-foot yacht, whose name he forgot, and his own shrimp boat, *Flying Dutchman*. Chief Toomer's *Si-Nan-Su* was one he helped rebuild when he was seventy.

"I built seven big boats," he said, counting them on his fingers. "They were good boats too. They didn't leak a drop of water. And when the bow went down in a heavy sea, she came back up. I'll tell you another thing," he added. "All the little ones I built were good for what I designed them for. And they didn't leak either. I did a lot of rebuilding too, and they held up, I tell you."

A boat's design depends simply on what she's going to be used for. Gerald said he could plan a speedboat—and did design many that raced between Key West and Miami—but you wouldn't be able to row her. Or he could design a rowboat—but you wouldn't be able to put a big motor on her.

Gerald liked describing the technique for softening wood for a boat's planks by steaming. The craftsmanship that goes into cutting boards for the deviation around the spiraling bow is easy enough "when you know how," he said.

"You bore holes in the plank. You always wedge into the grain, not sideways, or you'll split it," he said, using his hands as if to show an apprentice how to do it.

Gerald was born in 1898 in Tarpon Springs, Florida, to a family that made a living collecting sponges from the Gulf of Mexico and taking them by schooner to the market in Key West. They sculled dinghies and used twenty-foot poles and hooks until the Greeks came to Tarpon Springs and taught the locals how to dive to find the best sponges. That was around 1907, when Gerald was about nine years old.

In the flu epidemic of 1918, Gerald almost died. Three quarters of a century later, he recalled the sorrowful sight of ferries along Florida's Gulf Coast stacked high with the coffins of flu victims. During World War I, he worked in a shipyard in Jacksonville, worked at the U.S. Coast Guard station in Key West and married for the first time.

In the early 1920s he ran illegal liquor from the Bahamas to Florida in a twenty-six-foot boat and an airplane. By 1926 he had made enough money to open a club in West Palm Beach on New Year's Eve. But his marriage failed, so he left Florida to follow construction jobs to Texas and North Carolina, landing in the South Carolina Lowcountry in the 1930s, intending to make a living fishing.

For a while Gerald lived near the present site of the Chechessee River Bridge. From there he would row eastward with the tide ebbing from Point Royal Sound to Bay Point, around Fripp Island and Hunting Island and then catch the flooding tide to come back through Pritchards Inlet. Sometimes he fished the Hilton Head Island beach, at other times in the mouth of the Edisto River, rowing everywhere he went. In a 19-foot skiff with a 250-yard seine, 10 feet deep, he caught flounder, whiting, spot, bass, trout, shark and other fish that he delivered to market in Ridgeland. He recalled the price as twenty-five cents for six pounds.

Along with others in South Carolina during the 1930s, Gerald made a living by doing anything he could to make a dollar. One year he used two mules to farm a crop of tomatoes and corn for Bill Keyserling near Beaufort for one dollar per day wages. He "sawmilled." He cut and sold junk. "A lot of businesses went bankrupt during that time," he said. "I'd get the contract to buy the whole thing and cut everything up and sell it. Once I cut up a whole sawmill. The hardest thing I ever handled that way was a locomotive."

Gerald pointed with pride to projects and landmarks that he had a part in building. He listed houses in Beaufort and the utilities and the base for Parris Island's Iwo Jima monument.

Recalling that he never had a foreman to tell him what to do after he was nineteen years old, he said he almost quit a job in the shipyard in Savannah during World War II—embarrassed because he didn't know how to build a boat as big as those under construction there and didn't know how to build a boat out of concrete. After a while, he learned how to handle his section of each big project, and so he stayed on.

After World War II, Gerald Watkins built himself the *Flying Dutchman* for shrimping. "I loved it," he said. "Every time you pulled in the net, you'd have something different. Every time was exciting." The omens were in his favor. Every time he headed out to sea off the south end of Hilton Head Island, "a white bird" (likely a herring gull) he said, would meet him in the mouth of Calibogue Sound. A couple of "porpoises," he said, also met him out there to go shrimping with him and keep the sharks out of his net.

"I'd be pulling the net in and see an old shark with his mouth open, heading toward the bag where the shrimp were. Those porpoises would head him off every time. If it hadn't been for them, I'd have lost a lot of shrimp—and nets, too, probably."

When Gerald was eighty-three, he mused that he had come from a line of "long livers" and therefore expected to have a few more years to reflect on where he'd been and what he'd done. The times, he said, had "turned upside down," with inflation and interest rates in double digits and with girls running around all over the place in "little old bikinis." By then, he had retired from shrimping, and a stroke had curtailed his boatbuilding.

Gerald had married his fourth wife, Margaret, in 1972. A decade later, both of them had debilitating health problems. When I interviewed him at his home, he pointed to a whole table covered with patent and prescription medications. "That's $100 worth of durn stuff," he said, laughing. "But for me, a good visit and a little bit of storytelling can do more good than all of that."

Given the opportunity, he told plenty of stories about running liquor from the Bahamas during Prohibition, about fish and shore birds and about the long-lasting affection a man feels for the boats he's built.

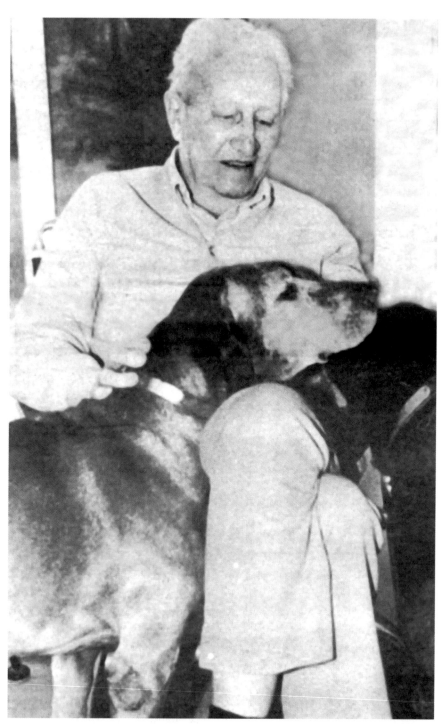

Laurence "Larry" Dunn.

DOES ANYBODY REMEMBER THE HURLEY HOUSE?

Laurence Dunn
Born in 1898

Once, he and some of the Hurleys' guests bogged a car down in the beach sand,
were taken home by a helpful farmer with a team of mules and then
had to use the mules to pull the car out—after it had been soaked thoroughly
during the next high tide.

In the 1920s, when the national economy was booming and the stock market rising, William L. Hurley owned a chain of ten-cent stores in Philadelphia and New York City. Wealthy enough to do as he pleased, he pleased to spend his winters on Hilton Head Island.

In January 1928, Mr. Hurley's family knew that as frail, ill and elderly as he was, he had only a few months to live—and that he was determined to live out his last days on the island he loved. So they hired Dr. Laurence "Larry" Dunn of Savannah, fresh out of his internship at New York City's St. Luke's Hospital, to move to the island to serve as Mr. Hurley's personal physician.

For Larry, a recent Harvard Medical School graduate, it was the duty of a lifetime. Mr. Hurley, his only patient, had two nurses to care for him. Larry was paid the unheard-of sum of seventy-five dollars a day. He had access to the recreational and social benefits of the wealthy.

Here is how he remembered the situation more than fifty years later:

> *Mr. Hurley was very ill and very pleasant. I stayed with the family in the big house to check him every day and give him medication. The Hurleys treated me like one of the family. I had access to the cars. They had two on Hilton Head—and a French chauffeur.*

They had a gamekeeper and were always having guests and parties and poker games. It was a beautiful place with servants and servants' quarters and guesthouses and plenty of good hunting. They had horses and dogs and people to take care of them. They had a yacht, which they docked in Broad Creek.

When I went with them to Savannah to social things there, they'd give me money to go out and have a good time.

DRIVING ON THE BEACH

There was plenty of time, most of the time, for the young doctor to hunt doves, quail and deer and to ramble over the island's woods and beaches, plenty of time to chase sand crabs and watch other wildlife in the woods and creeks. Once, he and some of the Hurleys' guests bogged a car down in the beach sand, were taken home by a helpful farmer with a team of mules and then had to use the mules to pull the car out—after it had been soaked thoroughly during the next high tide. Fortunately, the French chauffeur was able to get the car running again within twenty-four hours.

The Hurley House, as it was called then and for many years later, stood near the bank of Broad Creek on Otter Hole Plantation, a part of the 1,700 acres the Hurleys had been acquiring since 1898. It was a two-story house with brown wooden-shingle siding. An interior balcony overlooked a downstairs living area. With several bedrooms, two bathrooms, a spiral staircase and a screened porch, it may have been the fanciest house on Hilton Head at the time. Only the big house on Honey Horn Plantation came anywhere near matching it in size and grandeur.

Mr. Hurley lived longer than expected, from the end of January until the middle of April. He died one dark, rainy night. Using the only telephone on the island, at Honey Horn, Larry made arrangements for the body to be sent to Philadelphia. He, the family members, guests and servants prepared to transport it immediately to Savannah to catch the next train north.

The corpse had to be taken down a steep ramp to the floating dock to be put in the boat. In the rush to get it to the train in time, the crew carrying the improvised stretcher nearly dumped the corpse of Mr. Hurley overboard into the opaque waters of Broad Creek. "We had what I think we call a 'near-miss,'" Larry said later. "What a predicament that could have been."

Soon after Mr. Hurley's death, on earnings from about ten weeks of work on Hilton Head, Larry took two vacations, bought a car and furnished a doctor's office to begin a medical practice. He then treated patients in Savannah for forty-two years, frequently spending holidays, weekends and summers in Bluffton. He patched up Blufftonians in emergencies, talked them through sore throats and pneumonia and gave away samples of medication, although he never formally opened an office in Bluffton and never charged his Bluffton neighbors for his services.

As for the Hurley House, after modern development began on Hilton Head Island in the early 1950s, the Hurley House was briefly home to at least one other family. Converted to a nightclub later, it burned to the ground one night in the 1970s, leaving only rubble.

In 1972 Larry Dunn retired from his Savannah medical practice to live full time at Bluffton's Cedar Bluff, where Huger Cove meets the May River. He began to do a lot of fishing. Occasionally he recalled how lucky he was to be one of only a handful of people who could reminisce about the island as a rich man's playground in the freewheeling days before the stock market crash of 1929.

Thomas and Annie Fuller.

THESE TWO
PULLED TOGETHER

Thomas and Annie Fuller
Born in 1900

Eighty-one-year-old Annie had advice for her eighty-one-year-old husband: "If you trus' in the Lord, Thomas, he'll clear 'most everything out of your way. Don't worry so."

In 1981 Thomas and Annie Fuller were not sure when they fell in love, and it had been so long since they married, they were not sure how long ago the wedding had been either. Natives of Hilton Head Island, they lived in the tempo and rhythm of planting and harvest, ebb tide and flood tide, for more than eighty years, most of that time in the same spot, together, on the edge of Skull Creek.

Born in 1900, both grew up in the Pope community, both attended Mount Calvary Baptist Church and the Seabrook School, and both worked in the soil and on the creek banks. As for how they functioned together, Annie helped Thomas pick butter beans for the Savannah market for many years because, she said, with a smile, "You're supposed to pull together." Thomas said, with a loving glance at his wife. "When I married Annie, she had her health and strength. Now that she's not well, I'm going to do the best I can towards her."

The Hilton Head Thomas and Annie remembered as children was cleared from Braddock's Point on the south end to Elliott Beach on the north end and was heavily farmed. The surrounding waters were full of sailboats and rowboats and heavily fished. Residents didn't lock their doors, simply because the community did not tolerate thievery. Grown-ups shared in the tending of the island children, who roamed freely from one cornfield to another. The proper raising of youngsters was looked on as a task big enough to involve as many people as possible, Annie said. Nobody had any cash to speak of, but everybody had food, shelter, clothing and other necessities, plus a friendly community to call home.

If the place sounds like utopia, that's because the Fullers remembered it that way.

A Livin' by the Sweat of the Brow

Although physically demanding and monotonous, late in life Thomas and Annie remembered that the work of their youth was not drudgery. Thomas had to cast a net to catch shrimp or mullet for supper, but he did not remember the casting as terribly hard. Winters, he picked oysters—thirty to forty bushels on a single low tide—for two cents a bushel, then three cents, six cents and finally twelve cents a bushel. Summers, he raised butter beans, corn, sweet potatoes and watermelons and hired sailboats to haul them to Savannah to market. Annie shucked raw oysters in the winter and picked crabs and shelled beans in summer, but she didn't remember those chores as onerous. Asked how many gallons of oysters she could shuck in a day, she said she could not remember the amount exactly, but she said without apology: "I just know I did the best I could."

The Fullers and other islanders in the 1920s, 1930s and 1940s raised big fat roasting turkeys for the Christmas holidays. The pens would be full until mid-December, when islanders would cage the turkeys and haul them by sailboat or steamer to Savannah.

"Turkeys brought good money," Thomas said, "good money. That's what we used to buy Christmas presents for the children."

The loggerhead turtles that lumbered up from the ocean to lay eggs during the summer—and that occasionally stranded themselves on the beach after injury—were a bonus for living on a barrier island. Many islanders treasured the eggs as tasty morsels to eat and to harvest for sale in Savannah. Thomas loved the turtles themselves. He said a turtle has different kinds of meat on it—some that tasted like beef, some like pork and some like chicken. "A turtle was a good find," he said.

In the 1980s Thomas and Annie felt in their bones the brunt of what was happening to their community once traffic began traveling over the bridges to the island in 1956 and growth took off. They liked the island better BD—before development.

"They're all kind of people here now," Thomas said in the 1980s. "You can't trus' a lot of them. They break in your house and everything. They're just now finding Hilton Head, and we don't know who they are. If they keep on coming, we've going to have too many and we'll have to ship some of them to Bluffton," he added, grinning.

On hearing such a statement from Thomas, eighty-one-year-old Annie had advice for her eighty-one-year-old husband: "If you trus' in the Lord, Thomas, he'll clear 'most everything out of your way. Don't worry so."

Georgianna Bryan.

We Made a Livin' Wid Mus'

Georgianna Bryan
Born in 1900

Decades later, when the humidity was high and barometer falling, that ironing shoulder acted up. Or maybe it was that musk-picking shoulder. Or maybe it was the shoulder that maneuvered the oyster knife or the hoe in the vegetable garden.

The best cash crop Georgianna Bryan ever knew grew wild in the woods of Hilton Head Island. It was musk, also called "deer tongue," a plant about the size of a head of mature Romaine lettuce. Musk grows low to the ground in rosettes. It sprouts green in May, matures in midsummer for picking and regenerates as it's harvested. It asks for no plowing, no planting, no hoeing, no fertilizing.

A croaker sack slung across her back, young Georgianna would search out the musk patches on the north end of Hilton Head in July, August and September. She would pick the leaves, stuff them into her bag and then lay them out to dry in the summer sunshine beaming into her backyard. When they were crisp and brown and fragrant, she would load them onto a sailboat to ship to Bluffton. Eddie Mulligan of Bluffton paid cold cash for the musk brought to him from all over the Lowcountry. In his "musk house" on the edge of Huger Cove, he baled it for shipping to manufacturers of flavorings, perfumes and fine-cut tobacco.

For Georgianna, as for others in the area, picking musk was one of only a few options for making money to buy shoes, rice and flour. For many years afterward, she remembered the fragrance fondly. Raising her head as if sniffing, and smiling, she said, "We made a living with mus' and put it in the closet to make the clothes smell good."

When the musk season was over in the fall, and the musk plants grew stalks with tassels and clusters of purple flowers, Georgianna, like others, turned to oystering to make cash. She shucked many an oyster, standing all day on hard floors. "The steam[ed] was the easiest, but the raw made the mos' money. It was some hard work, though."

Georgianna also worked as a laundress for Honey Horn Plantation. It was her job for several years to keep the tablecloths clean and pressed and to keep the hunting lodge guests dressed neatly. She washed the clothes and linens. She cooked the starch. She heated the iron on a wood-burning stove until it turned blue. She built up a skill for smoothing the collars and cuffs of men's dress shirts just so.

A FEW ACHES

Decades later, when the humidity was high and barometer falling, that ironing shoulder acted up. Or maybe it was that musk-picking shoulder. Or maybe it was the shoulder that maneuvered the oyster knife or the hoe in the vegetable garden. Whatever the history that affected Georgianna, she could recall the labor and feel the aches from it.

Born on Hilton Head in 1900, Georgianna was raised by a grandfather, a man she remembered as affectionate and quick-tempered. "He was good to we. He'd pet us. He'd bring us biscuit [cookies] from the store. We knew he loved us. This, though. He was left-handed, and when he hit you knew he meant business."

The little black girl living with her grandfather walked down Gumtree and Squire Pope roads to "Seabrook" on Skull Creek, where there was a school, and later to Honey Horn Plantation for lessons. Books and chalkboards were available, and a teacher was on hand, but for some reason, Georgianna said she "didn't learn much about reading, writing and 'rithmetic."

BASEBALL, SAILBOATS AND TURTLE EGGS

To make sure no one felt sorry for a poor child who hardly ever left Hilton Head, Georgianna told those who would listen about the good times as well as the hard manual work in her life.

"We'd follow the boys' baseball team and be out all day, whoopin' and hollerin'. Sometimes we wouldn't get home befo' dark. We loved that baseball on this island. I loved that sailboat too, when it would hit that breaker and bounce. I'd ride it and go up and down," she said, grinning.

And they dined with relish on loggerhead turtle eggs. "They're better eating than chicken eggs," Georgianna said, smiling. "After you boil them, the red part in the inside gets hard, but the white still stays soft. Just salt them down. It's too good."

At the age of eighty-three in 1983, Georgianna was still depending on her hands to lure a bit of cash into the house. "My check is not very large," she said. "I make a little change this way." She was sewing scraps of fabric together to make quilts to sell. For her, scrapping in various ways to make a living was nothing new.

Perspective on Birth Years 1901–1937

Were the first three decades in the twentieth-century southern Beaufort County's best of times or its worst of times?

The waters were pristine and full of seafood. The steamboats provided low-cost and reliable transportation between their ports of call: Savannah, Jenkins Island (to serve Hilton Head Island), Beaufort and Charleston. The churches and praise houses settled most disputes, and crime was rare.

And yet, it must have been overwhelming to become a bride at the age of fourteen and within ten years become the mother of four. It must have been lonely to tend remote lighthouses year-round, 'round the clock. It must have been depressing for a black man to try to take his family on a trip and find out there was no lodging for people of his race anywhere along the road.

By some measures, it was the best of times; by others, the worst. And those who lived through it boasted about how they overcame the difficulties and rejoiced in the joys they remembered.

"Right out of Dis Field"

Walter Green, born on Hilton Head in 1907, with much pride was still using his turning plow, his cultivator and his harrow on his farm just off Matthews Drive in 1982. Walter's parents, Mingo Green and Rosanne Murray Green, had fed, clothed and sheltered their brood of thirteen children by growing crops in that same soil. For cash, Mingo Green had raised cotton, baled it and hauled it by horse and wagon to one of the Broad Creek landings, where he loaded it into his sailboat. He then sailed the cotton to Beaufort, where there was a gin, or to Buckingham landing, where he loaded it—first by horse and wagon and later by truck—to take to a cotton gin in Estill.

Walter beamed when he said he and his wife, Annie Mae, a native islander like himself, never had a home anywhere but on Hilton Head. Through the years of isolation, they made island living work for them. Along with raising vegetables for market on his family land, Walter took a job for a while as a longshoreman in Savannah, staying there during the week, coming home on weekends. Another time he worked on a dredge boat in Florida.

For many an oyster season, he picked oysters for the Lowden factory in Bluffton and the L.P. Maggioni Company factory on Jenkins Island. He would anchor his sailboat in the channel, row his bateau to the muddy shellfish beds and start loading oysters. Between the soft creek and the hard factory floors, there was plenty of heavy lifting. "I'd t'row the oysters into the bateau, row the bateau to the big sailboat, sail up to the wharf and t'row them up onto the loading dock. It was a lot of doin'," he said, taking off his cap and rubbing his head as if recalling his oyster-picking days. "You can do a lot of things if you make up your min'."

Walter made friends with the island's early developers, Fred Hack and General J.B. Fraser, and followed Hack's advice to him to hang on to the property he inherited. He did, though, offer observations about how modern development changed the island community he knew as a child:

"Peace is gone. Whenever whites and blacks want the same property, the whites always end up with it. The stealing came when the roads got paved. This place used to be a place of trust. Now if your car breaks down, you'd better get it home or they'll get your tires and battery. In the olden time you didn't have to put poison on the vegetables. You'd almost never see a bug. Now they'll eat everything up if you don't dust them."

One aspect of his farming had improved, however, as a result of the island's population growth that started in the 1950s. "There's no more hauling to Savannah. As long as I can make it, people will come right to my house to get it." He also sold his fresh vegetables to one local restaurant and one local hotel and bragged: "A lot of people eat food from right out of dis field."

So were the times the worst or the best?

That depends on whom you ask and when you ask.

"You Can't Be Scared of Work"

Charlie Wiggins, born in 1900 in Florida, was working on a U.S. Army Corps of Engineers dredge in the Intracoastal Waterway in 1930 when he stopped off at Hilton Head Island and decided to stay. He married Julia Singleton, born in 1904 on Hilton Head, daughter of a family with a lot of property fronting Broad Creek. To Charlie's surprise, he found it hard as an outsider to fit into the close-knit community. Looking back, he said, "The people wouldn't give me any jobs. They gave them to those who were born on Hilton Head. But I make it anyhow. The Lord help me. I sold a little mullets and crab. After while, I got a little carpenter work. I'd plant beans and take them to the [Savannah] City market."

Later, Charlie Wiggins became a master oysterman. He said that when the steam factories were running, he could, with his tongs, load as many as one hundred bushels of oysters on a single low tide. Once, he boasted, he and three others loaded 750 bushels during two tides.

That much oyster loading was possible only under certain conditions. "First," Charlie said, "you got to get where they is. Pick your place, where they is plentiful. They you got to work. You can't be scared of work or you can't do it."

As for Charlie's other ways of making a living, there were days when mullet were hard to round up, of course, and seasons when bean bushes needed rain that did not fall. Charlie and Julia had to learn to deal with a fluctuating income. "Sometimes you would be disappoint[ed], and you just have to catch up, maybe, the next time. You had to save your money you made, not waste. On the crabs, I'd make forty or fifty dollars in one day and then nothing. You had to work it out to make the cash last."

From their waterfront home on the same land Julia's father had farmed almost a century before, by the 1980s Charlie could look out at the developing elegant Shelter Cove village across Broad Creek. He understood the need of people to be near the tidal waters and get out into them, whether in a hundred-foot yacht or a twelve-foot bateau. In that respect, Charlie Wiggins, who settled on Hilton Head in 1930, was not very different from those who settled on the island much, much later.

In the years in which the next thirteen storytellers were born, the United States took control of the Panama Canal, and European settlers moved into Alaska. The film *The Great Train Robbery* began entertaining Americans in the cities big enough to have movie theaters. Albert Einstein formulated his theory of relativity. London hairdressers began giving permanent waves. World War I began and ended. *Winnie the Pooh* was published.

Most of the folk who lived in the southern section of Beaufort County lacked connection to most of the rest of the world, the nation and even the state; they lacked knowledge of what was going on elsewhere.

Such isolation was in some ways stifling and in other ways splendid.

Mary Jane "Janie" Gadson Brown.

ALBERT RAISE ME, BUT BOTH OF WE WAS BOSS

Mary Jane "Janie" Gadson Brown
Born in 1903

"I took to praying like I'd never prayed before. I asked the Lord
to take the heavy end and give me the light end."
The Lord did take the heavy end, and her prayers finally brought peace.

Mary Jane "Janie" Brown "didn't get no learnin'" from books, she said, but she got plenty from experience. In 1985, at the age of eighty-two, as the matriarch of a family spread from New York to California, she possessed a universe of understanding based on life's dramas, one following the other as steadily as ebb tide follows the flood.

Janie knew well what it was to bend her back over butter bean bushes all day, sort the beans in their hulls all night and collect fifteen dollars for her work the next day at the market. She knew about having to take a boat, a horse or shoe leather everywhere she wanted to go. She was a renowned expert in making a dollar stretch, in quieting the baby's crying, in getting answers to prayers.

Almost from the time she could stand, she used her small hands to rock a chair or a cradle for one smaller than herself: "I was the youngest, and my mother pet me, so whenever I wanted to I could just ask mama to let me take care of somebody's baby. I started that, and I didn't ever go to school."

A BRIDE AT FOURTEEN

Growing up playing in the oyster-shell street near Bluffton's oyster factory, Janie met one of the young oyster shuckers from Pinckney Island. Albert Brown was twenty-five and Janie was fourteen years old when they were married in 1917. They lived together for fifty-nine years, until he died in 1976.

About that marriage, "Albert raise' me," Janie said, laughing, "but both of we was boss." The babies started coming shortly after Janie moved to Pinckney Island with Albert—four babies born in ten years. Albert kept busy raising cotton, corn, peas, beans, sweet potatoes and watermelons for Savannah markets in spring and summer and picking oysters in fall and winter. He had his own sailboat, a "mother ship," to which men rowing oyster bateaux brought their muddy harvests for transport to the oyster factory. Janie kept busy with the babies.

Janie never especially liked island living, though, and was thrilled when she and Albert had "gathered up enough money" to buy about fifteen acres in the Buck Island area in 1927 and build a house there. There they had five more babies, and there all nine of their offspring grew up.

As for how Janie and Albert supported that big, rambunctious family, Janie said simply: "He was a working man." As the babies got older, and the older children began to look after the younger ones, Janie also jumped into farming to help Albert.

"We worked together. I would knock off in the field after all day and come in and feed the children and give them a bath. It was hard, but I had a strong back."

SORROW KNOCKS AND ENTERS

Making a living was tough. And yet, hoeing cotton and feeding and bathing children were small challenges compared to others Janie faced later. She lost a son to the Korean War, lost a son in a car wreck, lost a son in a murder, lost a daughter in sudden illness during a Christmas season. All of them were adults by the time they died, but their adulthood did not relieve Janie's grief over the loss of her children. With no professional counseling available in that place and time, with no tranquilizers to settle her nerves, in the absence of therapy to talk through her problems, Janie turned to her religion for comfort.

As a child, Janie had been rowed from Buckingham to Jenkins Island by her older brothers for occasional communion services in the Mount Calvary Baptist Church on Squire Pope Road on Hilton Head Island. As an adult, she worshiped God at Zion Baptist Church in Bluffton. In her mind, all her life, if the Lord never scolded, it was a sign that "you ain't prayin'." Tragedy in her family was a signal from the Lord. Still, it was tragedy, and it was sad, at times almost unbearable.

Once, after the loss of one of her children, Janie found herself unable to eat, sobbing at the supper table. From Albert, her husband, who didn't belong to any church, she got wise advice based on what he knew about her and her faith. He told her to pray.

"I took to praying like I'd never prayed before. I asked the Lord to take the heavy end and give me the light end." The Lord did take the heavy end, she said, and her prayers finally brought peace.

FAMILY GATHERINGS

At Gadson family reunions, for many years relatives from several states converged around Janie. Nine children produced many "grand" for her, plus "great-grand" in her lifetime. And they had scattered widely from Bluffton. Her oldest daughter, Katie Frazier, left home for New York in 1938. Two daughters and one son eventually worked in New York, so they gave Janie the train fare to visit them several times. She saw the city, marveled at it and knew instantly that she had to go back home to live. She didn't do much traveling otherwise. Her descendants came to her.

Geographically, at the end of her life Janie lived less than a mile from where she was born. She embodied the truth that nothing much happens in small towns, except birth and work and death. Nothing much. Except is there anything in the universe more significant than an infant with an umbilical cord still attached, anything more important than earning one's daily bread, anything more powerful than the passing of a loved one? Is there a better skill in all the world than the ability to quiet a fretting baby?

Naomi Wright Frazier.

Polish That Lantern

Naomi Wright Frazier
Born in 1905

After Naomi married, she reared her own family and finished out her last days very close to where her grandmother, a former slave, was crabbing when "peace was declare'."

In the nineteenth and the early twentieth centuries, ships hauling cotton, timber and other goods, along with passengers, depended on South Carolina's coastal lighthouses to show them where to go and keep them from running aground. The lanterns' wicks had to be cleaned, the reflectors scoured, the kerosene tanks filled, the lanterns positioned just so. Ships' crews, their lives and property, depended on the lighthouses beaming their messages out into the dark ocean, and the U.S. government depended on the "keepers."

"You had to do it right, and you had to do it every day," said Naomi Wright Frazier, who did her share of brass scouring in the lighthouses of Parris Island, South Island (in Georgetown County) and Hilton Head Island. As the youngest of nine children of a lighthouse keeper, Naomi had assignments that made her the "second keeper" on those posts. Despite not knowing much about navigation, she said her father taught her that people depended on her. She came to consider her responsibilities as measurements of her integrity.

"You had to make sure no wasps built their nests in the chimney. The brass was supposed to shine like gold. In fact," she recalled, "the whole lighthouse was supposed to be spotless. My father kept a wet sponge in his hand all day long to keep off the dust and fingerprints."

Along with caring for the lighthouse property, the keepers recorded weather data, especially wind direction and velocity. At the time, the lighthouses had the only direct communication with the rest of the world from many of the nation's barrier islands—first the wireless radios, then the telephones.

A Job that Paid Cash

Lighthouse keepers in that era had some of the few jobs in the Lowcountry that paid regular wages. When Naomi was born on Parris Island in 1905, the U.S. Navy and Marine Corps had a small base, although most of the island was truly isolated. In 1910 the Wright family moved to the South Island lighthouse near Georgetown—then back to the Parris Island lighthouse in 1917.

By then, military activity on Parris Island had picked up, and transportation between the island and the mainland had improved. As a government employee, Naomi's father had a rice mill and a corn mill, and the family had plenty of grits and rice. They collected a toll for milling others' grain but shared their largesse with local children as well. Naomi's mother cooked cornbread in a "great big pan," Naomi said, because she knew there would be a lot of hungry mouths when food was being served.

"Many of the children on the island ate most of their meals with us because their families didn't have enough. They would pump the water and cut wood for us, so my parents would let them stay with us. Their folks seemed satisfied to leave them. That's just how it was.

"The county gave us three months a year of school, and the people put up the money for another three months. That's the way we were educated." As a teenager, Naomi had the good fortune to be sent to Penn School on St. Helena Island.

Naomi remembered the Parris Island lighthouse as "six or seven stories" high. The lantern was attached to a track so it could be brought down and inside for cleaning, then winched back up every day. The hole for the wick's beam out into the ocean was in the shape of a man. Long after living on Parris Island as a child, Naomi could remember the sight of the little lighted man being cranked up to the top of the lighthouse.

When the federal government expanded its military base there during World War I, the settlement of blacks on Parris Island had to be relocated. The Wrights stayed on in the lighthouse keeper's cottage until 1921, when Naomi's father got the job of keeper of the Hilton Head Island lighthouse. Sixteen years old by then and very much a part of her father's operation, Naomi remembered 1921 to 1934 on Hilton Head vividly and fondly.

She described two lighthouses: the 136-foot lighthouse still standing in Palmetto Dunes Resort's Leamington Plantation and a smaller one in Shipyard Plantation. As Naomi described the equipment, just off the beach there, what was called a "beacon light"—a fixed, acetylene-burning lantern at ground level—"winked" to help ships' navigators keep their bearings.

GOVERNMENT INSPECTORS

The inspector came about twice every six months. We could hear the boats blow their whistles in Broad Creek. Four ships [steamers] *brought supplies to us. That's how Shipyard* [Plantation] *got its name.*

The ships were named Palmetto, Cypress, Mangrove *and* Snow Drop, *and when we heard the* Palmetto's *whistle, we knew it was the inspector coming, and everything had better be just right.*

My father would hitch up the horse and go get the inspector at the landing. He usually gave us a good report.

The signal system worked at least until 1934, when Naomi's father retired from government service. Both lighthouses were still going strong in 1926 when Naomi left Hilton Head for New York City. After working in a florist shop and enjoying the excitement of the city for about three years, she decided she really belonged on Hilton Head.

In 1929 she returned to marry Charles Frazier, a man handy with tools and horses and dogs. He worked on Otter Hole Plantation for the Hurley family and, in later years, for Honey Horn Plantation. Naomi and Charles reared seven children. To supplement their income, she made floral arrangements for weddings and funerals, using plastic flowers most of the time because she had no way to keep fresh flowers. For brides or grieving families unable to afford what she sold, however, she made flowers out of paper and gave them away. She saw sharing as a way of life because of her mother—who always cooked a big pan of cornbread on Parris Island, realizing that hungry children other than her own would be hanging around when it finished baking.

By 1983 Naomi was widowed and was surrounded by family members and living on Spanish Wells Road, not far from her roots. She had reared her own family and was living out her last days close to where her grandmother had lived during the Civil War.

Naomi's grandmother, born into a slave family on Hilton Head, had been thirteen years old when the war ended. The story passed down in the family was that she had been crabbing in the creek when "peace was declare'" and that she remembered "hooting and hollering" and dancing from house to house to celebrate.

As for the lighthouses Naomi remembered, the Shipyard lighthouse and beacon eventually succumbed to the erosive ocean. During the development of Harbour Town, one lighthouse keeper's house and another similar house from the same property were moved to the south end of the island, where they were converted into a restaurant and a real estate office. The Palmetto Dunes lighthouse was still standing early in the twenty-first century.

Roger Pinckney X.

Well Driller, Dock Builder and Philosopher

Roger Pinckney X
Born in 1909

The Klansman parked his horse directly in front of Roger and his friends, blocking their view of the ceremony and the hoopla.

Trudging the marshes building docks for almost fifty years, Roger Pinckney X was shaped by the lay of the land he loved. Investigating violent deaths as Beaufort County's coroner for thirty-five years, he developed a strong sense of right and wrong and came to feel he understood the causes of accidents and violence. Drilling wells from the days of the early twentieth century when water gushed out as soon as the pipe hit the aquifer, he came to espouse a deep indignation over environmental assault.

When Roger Pinckney talked, a lot of people listened. Usually, they asked for more. Like all good preachers, Roger spiced up his "sermons" with stories. A lifelong Lowcountry resident, he spoke with the heavy sounds typical of South Carolina's old-time coastal dwellers. A "deer" was a "deah." A "gate" was a "ga-a-ate." "About" was "aboat." His accent was a Southern drawl, not quite Gullah but distinctly coastal South Carolina, distinctly Pinckney.

> *When I tell judges about the trouble they cause when they are lenient on crooks, I know what I'm talking about. Sometimes you've just got to lock people up.*
>
> *"I've scooped up young people's guts off the pavement. I've had to tell people their son was half on the slab and half on the bark of the oak tree down beside the road. I've been around death, and I know what causes death, and I'm conscious of safety.*

I knew somebody was going to get killed when they started the Hilton Head ferry [in 1953]. *There was a power line in a dangerous place, and I saw it and told them. Sure enough, it killed a man.*

Before Union Camp [Savannah-area paper mill now owned by International Paper] *began sucking up our aquifer, we had flowing wells. They started going salty. In the 1960s, we started bringing water from the Savannah River and treating it at the Beaufort-Jasper Water Authority plant.*

I told them in the beginning not to pump out of the aquifer to water the golf courses on Hilton Head—to use the lagoons. Now the golf courses, together with Union Camp, are pulling on our water supply, and we're getting salt into the [Floridian] *aquifer.*

"This water situation is something people are going to have to come to grips with," he warned in 1982. He was right, of course. Later, the island's golf courses began using treated sewage water for irrigation, and the community water for southern Beaufort County had to be brought from the Savannah River and the Cretaceous aquifer 3,832 feet deep.

Roger Pinckney X was born in 1909 in Colleton County to Roger Pinckney IX and Fraser Dickinson Pinckney. On the Pinckney side of the family, Roger would have to back up almost a dozen generations, he said, back to England to find connections with the Pinckney Colony and Pinckney Island Pinckneys. On his mother's side, he added, his family tree includes the same Frasers as those of Charles and Joe Fraser, early Hilton Head Island developers.

When Roger was one year old, the family moved to The Point in Beaufort and his father went into the business of building docks and bulkheads.

Ku Klux Klan Rally

Roger was but a teenager when he joined a throng of other whites in the streets of Beaufort one night in the 1920s to see the hullabaloo that was building around the Ku Klux Klan state convention. Some of the Klansmen in their pointed caps rode in open "touring cars." Some marched, their white robes flowing, red crosses painted on their sides, their faces masked except for eye holes. They set a cross aflame near the rostrum, where the parade ended.

To hear the speeches better, Roger and a friend pushed against the rope strung to hold the crowds back from the stage. That infuriated one of the Klansmen. He ordered them to move back. He then maneuvered his horse to stand directly in front of the boys, blocking their view of the ceremony and the hoopla.

In revenge, with a rubber band and a bent piece of metal solder, Roger's friend fashioned a slingshot, reared back and fired at the horse's rump. That was all it took for the horse to bolt straight toward the podium and break up the ceremonies.

"People hooted and hollered, and they never got that meeting back together," Roger said, laughing about it more than fifty years later. "I can't say that was the end of the Klan, but that was the end of that rally. I don't know that they ever had another one in Beaufort County."

While still in his teens, Roger began working with his well-drilling, dock-building father during the days not only of flowing wells, but also of windmills and hand pumps. He remembered "rams" as well, automatic water pumps activated by the aquifer's water pressure. "A ram would pump the water into the tanks in people's houses. You could hear them clicking at night. It was ram power, used especially on the high bluff of the May River."

In 1927 Roger went to the University of South Carolina intending to major in civil engineering until, he said, he discovered there were no girls in the engineering school. "I decided that wasn't for me," he explained, smoothing his hair as if straightening it to get some girl's attention. "There were plenty of good-looking coeds in fine arts, so I picked that."

After college, Roger worked in North Carolina for a couple of years, for the U.S. Coast and Geodetic Survey for a couple of years, contracted construction work in Beaufort and began assisting his father as Beaufort County coroner. After serving in World War II, he got seriously into the business of marine construction. After his father died in 1946, he became coroner on his own and held the post until the end of 1980.

Beaufort County residents had plenty of opportunity to get to know Roger and for Roger to get to know them. Through his business and his public service, Roger traveled to the far ends of the rural county. A connoisseur of history and folklore, and a fine arts major to boot, he collected tales and told tales wherever he went.

EARLY HILTON HEAD DEVELOPMENT

"We were drinking Old Crow one night during a three-day deer hunt the North Carolina Hunting Club was holding [on the present Palmetto Dunes Resort property] for Beaufort officials. It was just after the Hilton Head ferry started up.

"Somebody started talking about a bridge to Hilton Head, and I told them how to get it by setting up a board and a charter, selling bonds and having it designed and built, charging tolls and then turning it over to the highway department. That's what they did," he said.

Only a short time later, Roger said he was talking to The Hilton Head Company officials and seeing them cut timber everywhere, so he made a suggestion: "Why don't you save some of the trees on the waterfront? You might want to give or sell some of that waterfront property to some of your friends one day."

That's what they did, too.

There was one time, he said, that he should have taken advice instead of giving it. In the early 1950s, he was on a deer stand on Hilton Head Island about where Pope Avenue is now, when the late Fred Hack, early developer, stopped by in a Jeep and took him to see a few stakes on lots he'd surveyed on the beachfront.

"He offered me a lot on the beach for $1,100 and said if that was too much, he'd sell me a lot behind it for $350," Roger recalled. "But I was holding some property on St. Helena and couldn't make any money on it, so I told Fred Hack he was crazy as hell—that nobody was going to spend money for that sand."

Thirty years later, Roger noted that for that missed opportunity, if he could have invented a kicking machine, he'd stand before it every morning.

THIRTY-FIVE YEARS AS CORONER

As coroner, Roger dealt with many a gory scene and many a tragedy. For him, suicides and deaths among young people from drug overdoses were the most traumatic.

In the 1940s, when neither blacks nor women served on juries in South Carolina, Roger made judicial history on isolated Hilton Head Island. Moonshine drinking led to a collision on "dead man's curve" on U.S. 278 that killed three people. That same weekend a nineteen-year-old knifed a young man in the heart, also on Hilton Head.

"The thing was we had to hold inquests on four deaths all at the same time," he said. "Because of a shortage of eligible jurors, I asked for a woman to serve. Nobody had ever heard of it before. But she did it, and nobody ever questioned me about it later. I happen to like women myself," he said. "I guess it was all right."

Except for the time of his military service, Roger lived in Beaufort all his life. He built his home for his own family not far from his childhood home, on property overlooking the Intracoastal Waterway. Where else?

"I've got to be on the water or they'd have to put me in jail," he said. "There's no in-between," Roger said. "In the evening I like to be with friends and have some bourbon, and I've got to watch the sunset over the water. That's all there is to that."

Roger and his wife reared four children who, he said, made him proud. "They're smart," he said. "They didn't take after me."

And in addition to his wife, his four children, docks, well-drilling, deaths and history, Roger Pinckney had other interests. He enjoyed petting and polishing and occasionally driving a 1956 Bentley automobile, plush and shiny. He also enjoyed rooting azaleas and grafting camellias.

At the age of seventy-three, Roger had started thinking about writing a novel, a "good story about women and men and loving and working." He had the background in his head, he said, because of all the "characters per square inch" in the sandy soil of Beaufort County. "There are just a lot of real characters here," he explained.

None, he might have added, more picturesque than Roger Pinckney X himself, a man in love with the land, the water and the people in the countywide community he called home.

Sam Stevens.

Excursions with Cap'n Sam

Sam Stevens
Born in 1911

His five vessels had a total capacity of 946 passengers, and the music and partying earned Captain Sam's fleet the nickname "the boogie boats."

Sam Stevens was a little black boy in the Deep South in the 1920s when he started rowing a boat across the Savannah River and riding the steamers that hauled freight and passengers in regional waterways.

Sixty years later, besides an oil distributorship he owned five boats that could carry almost a thousand passengers, if loaded and put to sea all at once. The passengers could dine on everything from seafood Newburg to hamburgers and could dance away the day or the evening on trips to Jacksonville, St. Simons Island, Augusta, Daufuskie Island, Harbour Town and Charleston. By then, Sam knew—on a first-name basis—President Jimmy Carter, Burt Reynolds, Secret Service agents of the former President Richard Nixon, the governors of many states, the mayor of San Diego and dozens of other sports figures and celebrities who had taken his excursions.

Wearing spiffy, starched captain's uniforms, Sam Stevens looked prosperous, in charge, jolly and every inch "the captain." He never knew he'd get quite as far as he did in the business community, but he fell in love with the water the first time he stepped into a bateau. Even after more than thirty years of telling sightseers about the geography and legends of the rivers and creeks of Georgia, South Carolina and Florida, Sam still enjoyed the guided tour part of his operation. To Daufuskie Islanders, he had become a hero.

Sam was born in 1911 in Darien, Georgia, a shrimping community, and moved with his parents to Savannah in 1917. His father built and repaired boats for the

U.S. Army Corps of Engineers in a boatyard on Hutchinson Island. Before he was a teenager, Sam began rowing across the river after school to learn the skills of his father's trade—hammering, sawing, measuring and caulking the seams of wooden vessels.

STEAMERS TO BEAUFORT

For fun on Sundays, his family would occasionally take the steamers that hauled freight and passengers between Savannah and Beaufort—*Clivedon, Pilot Boy* and *The Merchant*. They would make stops at Daufuskie, Hilton Head and Bluffton to load and unload people, trunks, chickens in cages, clams in croaker sacks, rice, sugar, coffee, farm implements and any number of other items. The biggest freight customer was the Parris Island Marine Recruit Depot, which depended on boats at the time for most of its supplies.

On weekends, the steamers, also called "packets," featured live bands and meals as well as sightseeing trips down the Savannah through Ramshorn Creek, into the Cooper River, up Calibogue Sound, up May River, through Skull Creek, across Port Royal Sound, into the Beaufort River and back. The blare of the saxophone and the beat of the bass could be heard for miles around the marshes.

"I thought even then I'd like to own a situation like that," Sam said, looking pleased with himself, a man who had realized a dream come true.

Unable to afford such a boat early on, as a young man, Sam worked several years as a carpenter's helper, mostly on the underside of a boat hull. When a job in the survey department of the U.S. Army Corps of Engineers came open, however, he immediately began working on a boat that traveled the creek channels from Beaufort to Fernandina, Florida. "I like it on top of the water," he explained, smiling broadly. A surveyor's rod man and chain man, he helped measure depths so the Coast Guard could install channel markers in the Intracoastal Waterway. He learned a few things about shifting sandbars and mud banks and about how different boats respond differently to shoals. "The boat will tell you if a place is shoaling up. You've got to know the boat, though. Some will take the wheel from you and run to the bank. Some boats will run to the deep. It depends on the way the boat is built."

In 1941 the Coast Guard put Sam on a boat to help patrol the South Atlantic coast during World War II and to pilot the ships into and out of the Savannah River harbor. When he was discharged in 1946, he could have returned to the surveyor's job on the Corps' dredge, but he had decided by then he wanted to do something for himself. There were no blacks in the fuel oil business in Savannah. Sam took out a GI loan and bought some trucks and started selling fuel oil door-to-door.

He bumped into Jim Crow. Officials of the Savannah Housing Authority, which managed many of the projects in which fuel oil customers lived, tried to stop Sam from going into their complexes. After he protested, the authority relented by saying it would be acceptable for him to sell to his relatives who lived in the projects as long as he didn't try to sell to the other customers. Building up his business under those circumstances was tough, "but we struggled through it. We beat it down," he said.

While looking for his first fuel oil customers in the late 1940s, Sam was also remembering the good times on the old steamers and looking for a boat to buy. "Bear in mind that I had no money," he said.

Nevertheless, he found a sixty-five-foot, 125-passenger boat named *Visitor* in New York City. Her owners, replacing her for a bigger tour vessel to use in that harbor, wanted to get her out of their competition range, so Sam got *Visitor* for an attractive price. Along with two black doctor friends and with the help of a white insurance executive friend, he was able to get 100 percent financing from Savannah Bank.

OUTINGS TO DAUFUSKIE

"Savannah people were hungry for boating," he said. "We'd take them up and down the river and over to Daufuskie. The Daufuskie people were able to do again what they used to do—to come down to the docks and sell their crabs and fruits and chickens, and to get off that island."

Sam's boat ran on weekends, on Wednesday afternoons and Monday nights, opening up a world for many Savannahians and Savannah visitors. The Savannah Bar Association went out on *Visitor* once a year. The schoolchildren took field trips so many of them could see their hometown from the water for the first time.

In 1966 Sam sold *Visitor* and bought *Waving Girl*, more than twice its capacity, at 317 passengers. Church groups, civic organizations and convention planners found Captain Sam's boat, and he had plenty of business.

In the early 1970s he bought two boats that together could carry 255 passengers. He named them *Harbor Queen I* and *Harbor Queen II*. Later he bought the 24-passenger *Independence*, which he used briefly as a ferry to Daufuskie Island. In 1982 he added a 350-passenger vessel, which he named *Cap'n Sam*. His fleet of five boats gave him a total capacity of 946 passengers, and the music and partying on the excursions earned Captain Sam's fleet the nickname "the boogie boats." When the winds were right, the jumping rhythm and blues entertained boaters and everybody on the waterfront from Savannah to the May River.

From the mid-1960s until 1978, Sam also owned Stevens' Anchorage, a pavilion, dock and restaurant on the Cooper River on Daufuskie. In the early 1980s, he still had his oil business and still remembered how to caulk a boat's hull. But his real business and his first love was then the same as it had always been—taking people out on the water for fun. At the age of seventy-one, long after his days of rowing and of riding the steamers, he still had not had enough of looking at the marsh and the egrets and feeling the sting of salt spray on his face.

Fred Sisson.

KEEPERS OF LIGHTHOUSES

Fred Sisson
Born in 1912

In the days when raccoon coats were fashionable, raccoons were plentiful on Hilton Head, and Fred's father supplemented his salary by selling 'coon hides.

Fred Sisson's worn, tattered, yellowing documents, many containing the wonderful old penmanship of the 1800s, mostly in brown ink, contained bits and pieces of information about the glory days of lighthouse keeping on the islands of the Southeast coast. They included agreements, assignments, correspondence and supply lists involving the operations of lighthouses from Hilton Head Island to Amelia Island in the period from 1879 to 1924. They showed salaries and prices and concerns about weather—and the importance of provisions such as salt, bacon, coffee and cherry brandy for families living in remote places and doing essential tasks for the nation. Representing a significant part of the Sisson family history as well as the history of the region, the papers were scrambled together, loosely, in boxes—on their way, Fred said, to a more orderly file system.

Born in 1912, Fred came along behind the prime time of lighthouse keeping and so never was a keeper himself. His first job was cleaning fish, his second rigging steel, another putting gears into ships, another measuring the depths of the water from the May River in Beaufort County to Apalachicola, Florida, for the U.S. Geodetic Survey. As a retiree, he kept himself busy by mating on yachts, raising an organic vegetable garden, knitting and pouring lead for cast nets, assembling webbing for toddlers' swings and deep crab traps and knotting hammocks.

While I interviewed Fred at his home on Isle of Hope near Savannah in 1983, his hands tied string knots steadily as he made a crab trap.

HILTON HEAD ISLAND IN 1897

Fred's grandfather, Robert Sisson, was a Canadian Irishman who served in the Union army on Hilton Head Island during the Civil War. Deciding to stay on the island after his discharge, he worked as a watchman for the federal government's island property. When the lighthouse in what is now Leamington Plantation was finished in 1879, he got the job of lighthouse keeper at a salary of $560 annually. Along with maintaining the property, the tower, the house and the outbuildings, the post required meticulous cleaning, filling, polishing and lighting of the brass lantern.

A letter from the Commerce Department said Mr. Robert Sisson would be hired as lighthouse keeper and would "be held to a corresponding accountability." Gradually, the federal government had expanded its string of lighthouses. By the last quarter of the nineteenth century, mining and shipping to and from Beaufort and Savannah, plus passenger traffic, had created lively water transportation operations offshore and in and out of Port Royal Sound. Hilton Head's light beamed out into the ocean to range with the beam from the Hunting Island lighthouse as a signal for the approaching schooners and the steamers. That a ship's captain might not get an accurate signal and thus endanger his ship because of a failure on the part of the lighthouse keeper was unthinkable. Shoals could be deadly. A ship that ran aground on a shoal would be pounded to shambles by the relentless waves. At the time, there was nothing powerful enough to free a ship stuck on a sandbar.

In 1890, three years before the Great Sea Island Storm of August 27, 1893, the Commerce Department assigned Robert Sisson to the Bloody Point Lighthouse on Daufuskie Island. After the hurricane, Robert found the Daufuskie beaches washed up to one hundred feet inland and found the Bloody Point kitchen, storehouse and boathouse ripped from their foundations and damaged. Later, for the government's lighthouse inspector, Robert listed the provisions lost in the hurricane that needed to be replaced: 1 barrel of flour, 40 pounds of bacon, a half bushel of salt, 12 cans of roast beef, a dining table, a 141-pound sack of oats, 500 pounds of fodder and 50 pounds of lard, plus "46 head of fine chickens," among other things. He said he did not expect to be remunerated for everything but explained the necessity of keeping a horse—and thus the importance of the horse feed. He said he had to have a horse for hauling oil and other supplies; for getting to the "steamer landing," six miles from the lighthouse itself; and for helping to manage the problem of the nearest post office, seventeen miles away in Savannah.

A lighthouse keeper on Hilton Head, on Tybee Island and on Hilton Head again for more than thirty-five years, Robert Sisson also took temporary assignments to serve as reading clerk for the South Carolina Senate and as secretary to the South Carolina adjutant general.

Robert's son, Charles, became a lighthouse keeper in 1892 at Venus Point on the Savannah River. When Fred was born, Charles was keeping the lighthouse on Amelia Island. A year later, Charles joined his father on Hilton Head, where they were both employed by the Commerce Department. The two Sisson families lived in the two keeper houses on the property. (At the time they were located just at the bottom of the Leamington lighthouse; eventually they were moved to Harbour Town, where one became a real estate office and the other a restaurant.)

RECREATION AND ENTERPRISE

Many decades after his childhood days at the Hilton Head lighthouse, Fred Sisson still could enrich the official information in his yellowing documents with stories pulled from his memories. A mischievous boy, he dropped live chickens from the top of the Leamington lighthouse, 136 feet up, so he could watch them flutter and try to fly before hitting the ground; miraculously, they did not die, he said, but merely lost their ability to cackle. From the beach, Fred, his siblings and friends gathered loggerhead turtle eggs by the "wagon loads" to sell in Savannah for a penny apiece. In the days when raccoon coats were fashionable, raccoons were plentiful on Hilton Head, and Fred's father supplemented his salary by selling 'coon hides. Wild hogs also were plentiful, so instead of raising pork, the family ate tender, juicy wild hog meat.

When it was time for Fred—the oldest of four children—to start school, there was no school for white children on Hilton Head Island so his mother rented part of a house on Isle of Hope near Savannah during the school term. Within the next year, 1919, the school at Honey Horn opened, and the whole family was able to live again on Hilton Head.

Three years later, the Commerce Department transferred Fred's father, Charles, to Daufuskie Island's Haig Point lighthouse. It was a time of a thriving population on Daufuskie, and the Mary Field School was going strong. Many residents held government jobs on the U.S. Corps dredges at work on harbors up and down the coast and at the quarantine station in the mouth of the Savannah River. Oystering was also a big business for Daufuskie Islanders in those days, but the biggest business of all, as Fred recalled Daufuskie in the 1920s, was "moonshining."

"There wasn't much farming on Daufuskie, not like there was on Hilton Head," Fred said, "but there were plenty of stills."

In 1924, when the Commerce Department closed the Haig Point lighthouse, replacing its kerosene-powered signal with stationary gas beacons in the sound, the Sissons were transferred to the Ponce de Leon lighthouse near Daytona and then to the Mayport lighthouse in the St. John River. The last stop on Charles Sisson's lighthouse tour of duty was what Fred called the "girl's house," the Elba Island station in the Savannah River.

Although lighthouse keeping folklore is common enough from Maine to Key West, probably no lighthouse resident has become more famous than Savannah's "waving girl," Florence Martin, a lighthouse keeper's sister who allegedly waved for decades trying to contact the lover she hoped would see her from an incoming boat. Florence was later immortalized in bronze in Emmett Park off River Street and was honored as well by the name *Waving Girl*, given to various boats that plied local waters.

Although Fred never actually knew Florence of the legend, he felt he knew her because of the story and because of his own days of gazing over the waters, watching ships and boats and dolphins and tracking the changing colors of the sky and the surface.

Beginning in the 1920s, markers, fixed buoys and lights on pilings were found to be less expensive to maintain than full-blown lighthouse-keeping services in the nation's most remote places, many of them on islands. Eventually the proliferation of cars created a demand for bridges, and vehicular traffic replaced water transport for cargo and passengers. The great era of lighthouse keeping—and the romance that went with it—ended.

Arthur Frazier. *Courtesy of Arthur Frazier.*

Didn't Have to Lock Up

Arthur Frazier
Born in 1914

He took off from his job long enough to march with Martin Luther King Jr. on Washington in August 1963, one century after the Emancipation Proclamation freed his grandparents from slavery.

Unpenned hogs, free-ranging chickens and turkeys, untethered milk cows and beef cattle roamed Hilton Head Island's farming neighborhoods from mid-November to mid-March every year. The animals, essential material assets of every family, got along with one another and found plenty of forage in the fields and woods. Everybody fenced in the winter gardens of collards and turnip greens to keep them from being trampled, and the system worked. Each livestock owner had his "mark"—a certain kind of toenail clipping for the poultry, a certain kind of cut on the ears of the four-legged animals. It was easy enough to tell who owned each cow in the herd.

"They didn't 'mix up' much, and when they did, we could straighten them out," said Arthur Frazier. "They didn't disturb anybody. Sometimes somebody would maybe steal a little something but not much. We lived very well on this island. There wasn't much cash, but we didn't need much. We all had big farms, and we didn't have to lock up a thing."

Even in that easygoing environment, Arthur learned the value of doing a chore the hard way if the hard way was the best way. Born on the island in 1914, early in his life he became the official maker of the fire in the school's pot-bellied stove—because the schoolmaster discovered that young Arthur always removed the ashes before starting the fire and therefore produced the best blaze quicker than the other students. When he was thirteen, he got a job as a handyman on Honey Horn Plantation, cleaning the hunters' guns and boots—and building their fires.

Gradually, Arthur's duties at Honey Horn increased. One of the most enjoyable was preparing and serving elaborate midday repasts in the fields and forests. These dinners were no leftover salt pork stuffed in a biscuit. Sportsmen reveling in the luxury of hunting on the game-rich 27,000-acre island did not want to take the time away from hunting to return to the main house for meals, so the Honey Horn staff took the tables, chairs, linens, silver, charcoal pots, meat and potatoes and coffee to them. Later, Arthur remembered with pride and pleasure those picnics in the dove fields and near the deer trails. "We went out all over this island every day with that charcoal pot. It was a fine meal prepared on the spot."

A 1936 photograph of Arthur Frazier shows him in a suit, a vest, a tie and shiny shoes, with a carefully folded handkerchief in a breast pocket, a banded hat on his head and an official-looking scroll in his hands. Six years later, in 1942, he married Earline Campbell, also a Hilton Head native, daughter of a schoolteacher and a teacher herself. In 1943, when the U.S. Marines had a station on the land that is now Palmetto Dunes Resort, Arthur got a civil service job for a year, spraying the island's ponds and swamps for mosquitoes. He saved the government money he earned to go into business for himself.

A Boat, a Barge and a Couple of Trucks

By 1943 the steamers and other commercial boats that had hauled passengers and freight back and forth between the Lowcountry's islands and the mainland for more than half a century dropped out of circulation, one by one. The Houlihan Bridge had been built across the Savannah River. Works Progress Administration (WPA) workers had paved some of the Lowcountry's dirt roads during the Depression. There was less demand on the boats as more of them got into competition with one another. In the early 1940s, Hilton Head Island residents were isolated as they had not been for many years.

In 1944 Arthur Frazier bought an old forty-foot boat, *Vernon*, from the oyster and canning business L.P. Maggioni Company. With a barge and a couple of trucks, he set up a ferry operation from Jenkins Island to Buckingham and to Savannah. On daily trips, Arthur hauled all of Maggioni's oysters, as well as produce, clams, fish, crabs and people. He could take two cars at a time on the boat and trucks and other heavy equipment on the barge. Soon, the community found Frazier's operations indispensable.

When Frazier was notified of his draft in 1945, Hilton Head Islanders petitioned the government not to take him. On the basis of the transportation service he was providing back and forth across Mackays Creek and Skull Creek, he was exempted from military service.

In addition to transporting people and their goods, Arthur shopped for his neighbors. "Islanders," he said, "would listen to the radio to see where the bargains were in Savannah and then write out their orders, with the places written down, where I was to buy their stuff. I was running all over town for them. Sometimes they'd give me their beans and potatoes to sell and tell me to pay them in groceries."

Once, an island resident gave him a long list and said, "Please don't forget my order. We're out of everything. We don't even have salt." On his way home from Savannah, all the way back to Buckingham Landing, he realized he had forgotten that big important grocery order, including the salt.

"I turned around, called the order in from Bluffton and went all the way back to Savannah for it," he said. "I didn't get home until ten o'clock that night."

There were other problems with the ferrying that involved all kinds of passengers and all kinds of cargo. Occasionally people fell in the water and had to be rescued. Other times, people got stuck on one side of the ferry ride or the other and needed to cross but didn't have any money. Arthur said he "couldn't pull out and leave them standing on the dock."

Given the demand, the boat and barge were almost always overloaded, Arthur said, and the only reason there were no major accidents in the Frazier transportation line was that "God brought us over."

Arthur was warned that bridges between Hilton Head Island and the mainland would cut into his then-profitable business. He wanted to see those bridges anyway. The business of hauling and shopping for islanders had become a hassle. He was ready to get into another business.

Soon after the drawbridge opened in 1956, Arthur ended his ferry service and started hauling timber and pulpwood instead. From 1958 to 1968, he worked as a longshoreman in Savannah, again commuting every day.

Arthur Had the Dream Too

Arthur took off from his job long enough to march with Martin Luther King Jr. in Washington in August 1963, one century after the signing of the Emancipation Proclamation that freed his grandparents from slavery. He had to go Washington, he said, because when he had taken his family on vacation, he could not find a motel to lodge them or a restaurant to serve them a meal in all of the South. In Washington in the crowd, he had the privilege of hearing the famous "I Have a Dream" speech. He brought back to Hilton Head the ringing in his ears of the famous words: "We will not be satisfied until justice rolls down like waters and righteousness like a mighty stream."

"I had a good life on Hilton Head, and I didn't complain," he said, "but the civil rights movement was just necessary, and I had to be a part of it."

After a car wreck in which he lost a leg in 1968, Arthur started running the small store and gas station he'd had for several years already. After he and Earline took two exciting trips, one to Canada and one to Alaska, he kept a small globe near the bubble gum supply on his store counter. It helped him dream of the possibilities of future travel.

He didn't need anything in those days to help him dream of the really good old days on Hilton Head when he was in charge of firing up the heater in the schoolhouse; of staging the hunters' picnics; or of running his ferry, loaded to the gunwales with turkeys, pickup trucks and passengers headed to Savannah to shop for the island babies' shoes.

Randolph "Buster" Murdaugh Jr.

Your Honor, Please

Randolph "Buster" Murdaugh Jr.
Born in 1915

*As the region's population grew and the economy picked up, the criminals
became more sophisticated and better financed.*

For more than eighty-five years, anybody accused of committing crime in South
Carolina's Fourteenth Judicial Circuit—consisting of the five counties of Beaufort,
Jasper, Hampton, Allendale and Colleton—had to deal with one of the Murdaugh
boys of Hampton. There was Randolph Sr., a Hampton attorney elected to the
post of solicitor in 1920. Then there was Randolph "Buster" Jr., elected solicitor
in 1940, after his father was killed in a train wreck. Then there was Randolph III,
"Randy," who was elected solicitor in 1986 and then hired Buster as his assistant.
Randy ended the Murdaugh dynasty by retiring in 2005.

Buster was born in 1915 in Varnville—a farming community, sister town to
Hampton—the son of Randolph and Etta Harvey Murdaugh. After finishing
law school at the University of South Carolina, he returned to Hampton
County in 1938 to practice law; he also began assisting his father in the
solicitor's office—without pay. After his father's death two years later, Buster
ran for the job and won—and then ran again and again until he had been in
office for forty-six years. One man ran against him twice and lost both times,
and no one else ever challenged him.

When I interviewed Buster in 1984, South Carolina Attorney General
officials believed he had held the solicitor's job longer than any other elected
prosecuting attorney in the country.

During Buster's tenure, the Beaufort region went through the transition
from a place of poverty and sandy two-rutted roads—where most people

fished or farmed for a living—to a financially thriving region known worldwide for golf, tennis and expensive oceanfront resorts. The solicitor's office had to continue revving up the level and pace of his operations to keep up with new requirements coming down from state and federal court rulings about handling crime—and with a constantly changing environment. As the region's population grew and the economy picked up, the criminals became more sophisticated and better financed.

From Moonshine to Cocaine

In 1938 about half of Buster's work involved prosecuting those involved in producing moonshine liquor. Daufuskie Islanders, as Buster remembered the situation, had the most elaborate illegal stills. The crooks then quit moonshining and started selling cocaine—dealing in bigger markets and across more jurisdictions—and handling more money. In addition, thieves quit stealing hogs and went after jewelry, television sets and luxury automobiles.

Through all the changes occurring around him, Buster kept running for reelection, he said, because he enjoyed investigating crimes of all kinds. "When you've got a crime you have to look at the whole thing and then begin pulling out the irrelevant parts, piece by piece," he said, using his hands as if pulling trash out of a bag.

"Once you get rid of all the tangential stuff, then you'll find the solution right there, lying open for all to see," he added, spreading his hands as if to illustrate the word "obvious."

"When you know who did it and make the arrest, you just round out the evidence and plan how to present it to the court."

Antagonism Toward Offenders

Considering crimes' victims as well as going through the intellectual exercise of unraveling what had happened, Buster developed a personal as well as a professional antagonism toward repeat offenders and those he believed had committed murder or stolen other people's property. His jaw tightened when he talked. "We're going to do everything we can to stop murders," he said. "Yeah, I think the death penalty is a deterrent. And another thing: I'll be damned if I'm going to put up with a thief."

The small folding knife Buster kept in his pocket for many years helped him get a conviction against a man charged with sexually assaulting two Hilton Head Island women. The suspect left the weapon he'd used to threaten his victims at one of the attack scenes. Initials on it were those of a previously convicted "peeping Tom," a man who had served six months on that charge and also six months for housebreaking. Soon after officers found the knife, they arrested the man.

The defendant pleaded guilty to second-degree criminal sexual misconduct. The judge sentenced him to nine years in prison. Buster hung onto the knife. After a while, he started using it to clip his camellias when he walked in his garden. He called it a useful reminder of his personal responsibility for every criminal warrant issued in the Fourteenth Judicial Circuit.

In addition to working to get convictions, Buster claimed he did his best to throw out cases based on flimsy evidence, determined not to waste other people's time. One warrant that never got to the grand jury, for example, accused a jail inmate of possession of "contraband" in jail. The prisoner had been irritating the jailer. When Buster found the alleged contraband was a radio, however, he refused to proceed. "A radio is not contraband. Forget that," he said. Another time, a deputy charged two suspects with "safecracking" for allegedly vandalizing a mechanical dollar-changer at an automated laundry on Hilton Head. "In no way could that be construed to be a safe," Buster told him.

SURPRISES AND ONE RETRIAL

Buster's reputation said he had a rate of 90 percent success in getting guilty pleas or convictions in the cases he handled. From time to time, of course, both judges and juries surprised even Buster. "Sometimes I'd think we had a tight case, and they'd turn the defendant loose. Sometimes I'd think the defendant was guilty but wasn't convinced I could prove it, and the jury would give a verdict of guilty."

Almost humbly, Buster added, "I have to assume that the judgment of twelve people is better than the judgment of one. So even when I think the jury's done wrong, I don't worry about it any more, once the verdict is read."

After saying that, Buster had a second thought.

"One time I got a conviction of a black man assaulting a white woman, and the judge sent the man to the electric chair. After the trial I learned something I hadn't known before, facts that convinced me the man hadn't done it. I moved the court for a new trial and asked that the case be dismissed. It was the only thing I could do," he said, "and live with myself."

A FORTY-YEAR-OLD CRIME

Human nature didn't change over the years Buster served as solicitor, however, and the old reliable elements of physical evidence and persuasive witnesses continued to be the tools of the trade. Buster once prosecuted a man forty years after he committed the crime:

It's been a while now, but as I recall, a fellow was riding in his wagon when he was ambushed and killed. The fellow that did it left the state and changed his name and figured we'd forgotten about him and the crime.

But Ed McTeer [former Beaufort County sheriff] *kept the thing open, and when the fellow applied for Social Security forty years later, he had to produce a birth certificate, and we caught him that way.*

The man who had been riding in the wagon with the victim happened to be still living, so we had a witness, and we went to trial and got a conviction. I believe he applied for the Social Security forty years to the day that he killed the man in the wagon. That was a hell of a note, wasn't it?

By building up his law practice, buying land and selling it and investing in various small businesses, Buster became independently wealthy while prosecuting criminal cases. His wealth and his lack of fear warded off pressure from outside forces, he said. "Oh, I've been threatened. I've had defendants tell me in the courtroom, 'I'm going to kill you when this is over,' but I don't worry about them. I couldn't do my job if I worried about it."

Doctors warned Buster in 1975 to reform some of his workaholic ways, so he gave up his law practice and got his hands out of some of the businesses with which he had become involved—and started duck hunting more. He also began spending more time at his place on the Chechessee River.

In 1986 he finally decided not to run for solicitor himself but to support his son, Randy, in the election—and then to apply to Randy for the job of assistant solicitor. Randy served as solicitor until late 2005.

Buster thrived on criminal investigation and prosecution. He always spread a tense hush across the courtroom when he stepped up to the bench and announced confidently: "Your honor, please, the state's ready."

Thomas Holmes.

His Father Taught Him How

Thomas Holmes
Born in 1917

"Now some work with the tide on the plantin', but I work with the moon," he said.
"The crop seems to strive better for you if you do it that way."

Thomas Holmes still hung pork over hickory chips in his smokehouse under the chinaberry tree in his back yard on Hilton Head Island. In his front yard he still grew watermelons, corn, okra, peas, tomatoes and beans.

On Sundays and other special days he took a right turn at his gate on Gumtree Road to go to services at Mount Calvary Baptist Church on Squire Pope Road, where he was baptized in 1929 and where he became a deacon in 1957. Thomas liked being in a familiar place and liked doing familiar things.

Born in 1917, Thomas was the son of a native Hilton Head Island mother, Georgiana Wright Holmes, and a Daufuskie Island native father, James Holmes (after whom he named a favorite plow horse "James"). From the front porch of his home, Thomas could point to where he was born. He used the Gullah expression "all my days" to tell how long he had been living on Pope Plantation. He remembered well how his mother stirred bone marrow and lye into soap in a pot on a fire in the yard nearby. He could remember as if it had been the day before how, once in a summer thunderstorm, he raced lightning to a cow tied under a shade tree. He had hoped to move the cow for her protection, but he was too late. Lightning killed her.

Thomas's childhood was highlighted by sailboat trips to Savannah with his father to haul vegetables (pronounced "wegatables" with stress on the third syllable) to market. His father kept a twenty-five- or thirty-foot sailboat, the Holmes family cash-flow lifeline, anchored off a flat beach on the shore of Skull Creek. They rowed a bateau to it. The length of time it took to travel down

Skull Creek, across Calibogue Sound, up the Cooper River, through Ramshorn Creek, into the Savannah River and to the Savannah City Market depended, Thomas recalled, on "how the wind was breezin'."

"My father learned me how to sail the boat—when to slack 'em and when to pull 'em back een," he said. "Wit' a stiff win' straight behin', I could make it to Savannah in five hours. But if you ain't got no good win', it could take two days. It was mighty dangerous crossin' Calibogue sometime. William Ford—bless the dead—once had his mas' and sail overboard right off Brams Point. He didn't drown, but it was some time."

OXEN IN THE FIELD

Also from his father, Thomas learned to work oxen in the Pope Plantation fields. Like mules, he said, oxen "have plenty of sense." Thomas remembered this about following an ox pulling a plow: "He'll work from 7:00 a.m. until noon, but when dinner time comes, he'll lay down in the road if you don't stop for him to take a rest."

One more thing from Thomas's father: "I've done a lot of work. I'm not scared of work. Daddy told me if I have something I have to do, 'Go ahead and do 'em. Don't depend on somebody else to do 'em. You might get disappoint[ed].'"

For young Thomas growing up in the Lowcountry, it was not all work and no play. There was a society hall called the "Boys Pleasure Club" not far from Pope Plantation. On Saturday nights the community gathered for dances. While Thomas didn't dance, he used the occasion "to look them over."

And there was Skull Creek. When the sun was hot, Thomas and his friends would jump in "for cool off." Unlike many islanders, who knew only to fear the water, Thomas loved it. "I learn me own self to swim," he said.

Thomas also learned to string crabs together on a palmetto limb by first whittling the limb down, then wrapping the crabs' fins and claws around it.

After Thomas's father died, Thomas "step[ped] in" as a Hilton Head farmer with a reputation in Savannah. To increase his farm's yield, he bought fertilizer and pesticide from Savannah, but just to be sure he took another precaution: he planted, always, three days after the full moon.

"Now some work with the tide on the plantin', but I work with the moon," he said. "The crop seems to strive better for you if you do it that way."

Like many of his Lowcountry neighbors during the 1930s and 1940s, Thomas made his living out of the soil in summer and out of the creek in winter (on oysters). When he first began picking oysters, he could load up only ten to twelve bushels on a single low tide. At his peak, he said he could load as much as fifteen to twenty bushels at low tide, then haul them to the factory and unload them before going home to rest.

For a while, Thomas said he "threw dirt" on Beaufort County roads, earning wages of sixty cents a day. For a season or two, he headed shrimp in L.P. Maggioni and Company's big shrimp canning factory on Jenkins Island. He never tried to catch shrimp for money because, he said, he didn't like "foolin' with nothin' that runs" from him.

When Thomas and his wife, Mamie, were earning eighteen dollars per week combined, picking and shucking oysters for the Toomer factory on Jenkins Island in 1939 and 1940, they saved, in less than two years, enough money to pay the late Charlie Ulmer of Bluffton cash for all the lumber they needed to build a house. They hired a man to haul the lumber to the island and hired Mamie's uncle, a carpenter, to build it.

The high winds of the 1940 hurricane lifted the new house's roof, and the rains poured in.

"I jumped up and tried to get it back, but as luck would have it, it wrap 'round me 'most," Thomas said. As for how badly the storm treated their home, Thomas said simply: "It wreck 'em." He spent several weeks repairing the damage himself.

MONEY DURING THE WAR

During World War II, Thomas Holmes finally made some money. In 1943, '44 and '45, he took the night shift as a longshoreman on the Savannah riverfront. The pay was $13.50 per night for most cargo, $22.50 per night for workers willing to handle explosives.

As for the hazard of loading explosives onto a ship at night, Thomas dealt with it this way: "It was good money, so I cancel[ed] out the fear. The Lord go along with me on it."

Mamie Walters, who Thomas married in 1939, also was born and reared on Hilton Head. Together, they were a thrifty pair, in part because they didn't "bother with liquor or beer," Thomas said. They reared four children—Janie, Rosa, Valerie and Thomas Jr.—before Mamie died in 1970. Thomas said he had "never made much" but he had managed to "be careful with it [money]."

"And the older I get, the carefuler I is," he added, slapping his knee and laughing.

Despite the changes that swept over the island beginning in the 1960s, Thomas continued into the 1980s to follow the living patterns he learned from his father. He found it hard to adjust to the new economy. Sophisticated resort area real estate experts said at the time that Hilton Head's half-a-million-dollar houses were still a bargain in comparison to similar properties in Hawaii or Palm Springs, but Thomas was shocked at the price of a slice of beef steak in local supermarkets.

From the supermarkets' meat counters, he chose oxtails instead, from which he said he could make a "wonderful stew."

Albert Stoddard.

MEMORIES OF MELROSE

Albert Stoddard
Born in 1920

With affection and respect for the Daufuskie Islanders for whom Gullah
was the primary language, Albert Stoddard preserved the Gullah stories
in a way that everyone who could read English
could enjoy them.

To Savannah banker Albert Stoddard, Daufuskie Island's Melrose was
always much more than a piece of South Carolina real estate converted
into a golf resort. He grew up in Savannah, living with the porcelain and
silver his parents rescued in 1912 from the burning Melrose Plantation
house, listening to the soft sounds of Daufuskie Gullah performed by his
well-educated father and immersed in his family's keen sense of the value
of historic preservation. President of Historical Savannah Foundation for a
time, Albert said he saw "preservation as progress."

Albert's ties to Daufuskie reach back to 1740, when King George II
gave most—and maybe all—of the island to David Mongin in recognition
of his exploits against Spanish pirates. David Mongin planted long-staple
cotton and held out as a Tory during the American Revolution. The land,
reportedly producing an income of "opulent dimensions" by the early
1800s, eventually ended up in the hands of an orphaned granddaughter,
Mary Mongin.

The name "Mongin"—also spelled "Mungin" and "Mungen"—is preserved
in the name of the creek on the south end of Daufuskie that connects the
Atlantic Ocean and the New River.

SEA-ISLAND COTTON

In 1836 the Daufuskie heiress Mary Mongin, in a ceremony held at the American Embassy in Paris, married John Stoddard—a descendant of Jonathan Edwards, the well-known Puritan theologian and former president of what is now Princeton University. John Stoddard was a member of a Boston importing house, but, after marrying Mary, he directed his attention to planting cotton on Daufuskie. According to an early writer, his judicious management of the properties almost tripled their value. John and Mary Mongin Stoddard left their several Daufuskie Island plantations, including the seven-hundred-acre Melrose, to their several children.

During the Civil War, Union forces occupied Daufuskie, but the Melrose mansion, built in the first half of the nineteenth century, survived intact. In the late nineteenth and early twentieth centuries, the Stoddards continued to plant cotton successfully.

Albert Stoddard the planter—father of Albert Stoddard, the banker, whom I interviewed—was born in 1872. He grew up in the Melrose house with his widowed father, never attending elementary or high school. After being tutored at home, however, he went straight to the University of Virginia. In Savannah and in Bluffton, he was known as the islander who came to parties under his own oars—literally—by taking advantage of the incoming and outgoing tides.

According to the memories passed down through family members and a few old photographs, Melrose in those days was an imposing mansion of two stories on a tall brick basement and included a well-stocked library, a music room filled with fine instruments, marble mantelpieces, a formal garden loaded with roses and known by garden lovers from Savannah to Charleston, a boathouse, a gazebo and a barn.

During the hurricane of 1893, when saltwater covered much of the island, Albert was the only member of the family at home. He lay on the floor of the mansion's attic, convinced that, if the house should shudder on its way to collapsing, he would feel it first there and would be able to escape. Although the storm surge laid waste to the Melrose gardens and fields and eroded the bluff, the house made it through the hurricane with only minor damage.

A few years later, Albert the planter brought his bride, Evelyn Byrd Pollard of Virginia, to live with him and his father in the Melrose house. After the Melrose mansion burned, the family moved into the boathouse. Evelyn started the island's first post office—in the tack room at Melrose—but by 1918, the boll weevil had eaten its way over to Daufuskie's cotton fields. By then, Albert's elder son was ready for school. There were enough reasons for the family to

move to Savannah. Albert the planter became Albert the Savannah real estate broker, and the Stoddards never lived on Daufuskie again.

Albert the planter kept the land and small buildings on Melrose, and throughout the 1920s and 1930s, often caught the steamer *Clivedon* to visit his property and friends on Daufuskie.

Recordings of Gullah

Albert the planter-turned-real-estate-broker had learned formal English and math from his father and the patois of Gullah and coastal barrier island tales from his black friends and neighbors. In the 1940s, at the age of seventy-seven, at the request of the head of the Folklore Section of the Library of Congress, he went to Washington and recorded some fifty tales, thirty animal stories and twenty Daufuskie stories, all in Gullah.

Albert the banker, his son who was born in Savannah in 1920, followed his father to the University of Virginia before going to work for a Georgia firm making turpentine and resin and then working for thirty years for Savannah Bank and Trust Company. He and his brother held onto Melrose until 1972. Unwilling to develop the property but feeling they could not afford to donate it to the public, the brothers sold the land that year to a firm called the Bluffton Land and Timber Company, a group of investors, including the Frasers of Sea Pines and the Harrisons of Bluffton and Savannah.

Bluffton Land and Timber then sold it to the Daufuskie Island Company, a firm owned by two partners, one from Columbia and the other from West Virginia. In the spring of 1984, the Melrose Company—whose fifty investors were represented by three partners, Steve Kiser, Jim Coleman and Robert

Kolb—bought Melrose. Through an innovative marketing technique, they developed it into a "national country club," a members-only organization of golfers and beach walkers who reveled in the mystique of owning a piece of an antebellum plantation.

After retiring, Albert the banker took on a labor of love. He translated the Gullah stories his father had heard as a child on Daufuskie and then recorded in the 1940s for the Library of Congress into standard English and published them—with the Gullah on one page and the English on another beside it. With an easy-to-use translation, Albert explained, readers who had never heard Gullah spoken and for whom the Gullah they had heard was a mystery would be able to understand and enjoy the dialect.

At his home on West Gordon Street when I interviewed him in 1985, he gave me an example of one of the Gullah axioms he liked so much—and a story to illustrate its truth.

"E's a po' man ef e ain' got no escuse."

After a hurricane damaged a church on Daufuskie, one of the members, less than a skilled carpenter, was asked to make repairs. He did the work, but when the committee inspected, one of the members said to him:

> *Bredder, you done uh berry good job yuh, but us tink da cornder sort uh swag ober leetle.*
>
> *No, Suh, Bredder, da cornder ain' swag over none tall.*
>
> *Yet, Bredder, uh tink e swag ober leetle.*
>
> *No, Suh, Bredder, da cornder ain's swag none tall. Uh'll get one plumb line to show you.*
>
> *When the plumb line showed a lean for sure, the deacon said, Enty uh tell you say da cornder swag ober?*
>
> *No, Suh, Bredder, dis cornder ain' swag ober none tall. Dis duh one berry old plumb line, suh, en e's onreliable.*

As Albert recalled, "E's a po' man ef e ain' got no escuse." With affection and respect for the Daufuskie Islanders for whom Gullah was the primary language, Albert Stoddard preserved the Gullah stories in a way that everyone who could read English could enjoy them.

In 1995 Push Button Publishing Company published *Gullah Animal Tales from Daufuskie Island, South Carolina*, as told by Albert H. Stoddard, illustrations by Christina Bates, translations and editing by Will Killhour.

Mary Graves.

Big Family, Big Adventures

Mary Elizabeth Graves
Born in 1921

Bluffton was wonderful, but you had no idea what was out there in the big world
if you didn't get out of Bluffton and see something else.

Despite her deep roots in the Lowcountry soil, Mary Elizabeth Graves spent forty years away from Bluffton for college, military service and a career in physical therapy. When she retired, she settled back into the early twentieth-century New England–style house on Calhoun Street, where she had been born and raised.

Among other papers stashed away in the home of her birth, she discovered a handwritten Bluffton town ordinance that her grandfather, "George Sewell Guilford, intendant [the town's first mayor]," had signed in 1903: "It shall be a misdemeanor to block the sidewalk, foot path, lane or any public way. Either by horse, mule, ox or any animal whatsoever, either by cart, wagon, buggy, carriage, gig or anything that may be an impediment to pedestrians. Nor persons congregating or loitering." The penalty was to be a fine of one hundred dollars or thirty days in jail. As a retiree in her hometown, Mary Graves became the leading spokesman on behalf of public rights of way in the Town of Bluffton.

Guilford and Graves

Mary's grandfather, George Guilford—offspring of a Maine shipbuilding family—after serving in the Union army on Hilton Head Island during the Civil War, moved to Jasper County and then in 1888 to Bluffton. Mary's mother, Cora Jane Guilford, spent the last years of her childhood—as well as the rest of her life—in

Bluffton. Mary's father, John Samuel "Sam" Graves, grew up in the Okatie area. Mary was one of the eight children Cora and Sam reared in Bluffton.

An entrepreneur, Sam owned a store and a cotton gin and, at one time, a bank on Calhoun Street. He bought and sold real estate. He handled lime stock, a stark-white product of Lowden's big oyster-shell mill on Bluffton's Verdier Cove—used in chicken feed to strengthen eggshells.

The family lived for a few years in an apartment over Sam's store. Then Grandfather Guilford designed the New England–style house for the growing family, and Sam built it on Calhoun Street in 1915. Cora and Sam's eight children had a dozen cousins, the offspring of Aunt Maude and Uncle Jesse Peeples, living just down the street. More cousins, the offspring of Aunt Gertrude and Uncle Jack McCreary, lived on the edge of Verdier Cove in a house overlooking the Lowden oyster factory and shell mill.

"I know there's never been a family with more love in it than mine," Mary said later in life. "My mother was so loving, such a diplomat, such a wise woman. And the house was always filled with music. It made people feel good to be in it."

SPORTS AND COMPETITION

At the age of two, Mary learned to swim when the high tide covered the sandy white beach at the end of Calhoun Street. At the age of three, she and her cousin Mildred Peeples ran away to the bathhouse to strip off their clothes and paddle about at the river's edge, just the two of them. A spanking from her mother for that jaunt didn't keep Mary from doing the same thing again. It had been an adventure, and adventures attracted Mary all her life.

Although most girls in that community at that time found little pleasure from being athletic or competitive, when Mary was a little older, she and cousin Mildred followed her brothers and cousins and the other Bluffton boys, climbing trees, swatting at softballs with broomsticks and playing "Honey, Honey, Haro," a hide-and-seek game played on bicycles. By the age of ten, she was playing tennis on an oyster-shell court on the school grounds. "I was a tomboy," she said. "I had to have challenges." In an old barn in town, she and her playmates built a trapeze and a tightwire to play circus. "It's a wonder we didn't get killed," she said.

Mary's teenage years meant adventures in the May River, dancing to live music at Johnny Harris Restaurant in Savannah, a view from her backyard of Amelia Earhart's plane on its final flight and Saturdays working in a store on Calhoun Street from seven in the morning until ten at night to earn one dollar a day.

Unlike most children who grew up in the isolated culture of southern Beaufort County, Mary had the good fortune, after graduation from high school in 1938, to spend six weeks in New York City with friends of the family. The World's Fair and the sights and sounds of metropolitan New York in 1939—urban street life, museums, theaters, restaurants, subways, taxis and books, books, books—meant a plethora of new experiences for her.

"New York was an eye-opener," she said. "Bluffton was wonderful, but you had no idea what was out there in the big world if you didn't get out of Bluffton and see something else."

Mary credits much of her budding ambition and motivation to that New York trip. After two brief starts in college, at the age of twenty-one, she entered Winthrop College, where she majored in physical education.

PHYSICAL THERAPY CAREER

In the early 1940s, the times were a-changin', and Mary was ready to change with them. Having reveled at the age of three in an escapade or two to the river, Mary reveled in new challenges in her twenties. Just as she was looking around and just as World War II ended, thousands of injured war veterans and thousands of polio victims needed rehabilitation. The field of physical therapy was about to take off. Responding to a government pamphlet designed to recruit therapists, Mary embarked on her life's work.

Perhaps she was drawn to health care, she said later, through her memories of her grandmother, "Doctor Guilford," who treated ailments and injuries in the Bluffton area in the early 1900s. "I guess the laws about licensing were slack, because my grandmother had no medical degree, nor was she a nurse," Mary said. "In at least two ways she was ahead of her time, though. She used pressure points on certain areas of the body to relieve pain. Also, when an open wound did not heal quickly, she would mix a little bit of bread mold in her compound. It may have been similar to penicillin."

Mary crammed a two-year course in physical therapy into one year—six months at White Sulphur Springs, West Virginia, and six months in Galesburg, Illinois. "I'll always be grateful," she said, "to my government for opening doors for me that I had never dreamed of." Mary joined the army as a second lieutenant, and soon was serving in a hospital on Clark Field in the Philippine Islands and then in Naha, Okinawa. Later, in 1947, the little girl who had spent most of her life barefoot in the streets of Bluffton, vacationed in Shanghai.

After her discharge as first lieutenant in 1948, Mary served in the army reserve until her discharge as a captain in 1956. Her civilian career for the National Foundation for Infantile Paralysis took her to California, Oklahoma and North Carolina. After graduate studies at New York University, she went into independent physical therapy practice. In 1970 she became president of Graves and DePuy Physical Therapists, Incorporated, in Charlotte. She retired in 1982.

"The various medical problems we worked on included injuries, of course, but also strokes, Parkinson's disease and other neurological disorders. We worked in orthopedics and worked on a lot hand cases," Mary said. "It was our job to not think about ourselves but to think of the patients. It was hard work but rewarding work."

A Patent

Mary invented an electrical and hydraulic device to provide automatic passive motion to the ankle joint for therapeutic stretching of the heel cord. After perseverance with engineers, patent lawyers and the Underwriters Laboratory, she was awarded a patent in her name in 1971.

Mary and her staff always functioned, she said, according to her personal original philosophy: "To always be cognizant of the inherent worth and dignity of all persons. To remember that we are not all created genetically equal and because of this there will be many varied intangibles encountered in each individual to which we must adapt our professional knowledge and personalities in order to provide the patient with opportunity to obtain his maximum performance."

Proud of her profession and happy in her work wherever she was, Mary never forgot the people and the hometown she loved. From the Philippines, she kept in touch with Bluffton via ham radio. From other locations, she wrote home, called home and visited home often.

She had a special rapport with her oldest brother, Junior—the entrepreneur who leased and then built an oyster factory in Bluffton, built a crab-canning factory and raw-shuck oyster factory on Trimbleston Plantation and also ran oyster factories on Daufuskie Island and Jenkins Island in the forties and fifties. "Upon his return from college in 1932, Junior got into the oyster business because, really, there was nothing else to do in Bluffton to make money. He did well," she said. "From time to time, practically the whole family helped him in the oyster business, and the family was in the seafood business until 1968."

Mary also had a special connection with her father. On the porch that wraps around the Graves house, Sam would sit in his old rocking chair with his feet propped up and a cigar in his mouth. From that vantage, in the era when the windows of both the United Methodist Church and the Episcopal Church of the Cross were flung open on all but the coldest winter Sundays, he could listen to hymns, prayers and sermons while gazing at the moss-draped live oaks. Sam was moved to reverence there, he told Mary, better than he would have been had he been sitting in the church pews.

Mary understood that. A non-participant in organized religion herself, all of her life she spoke of deep respect for the creator, for honesty and for accountability. She thought of Bluffton's openness and its scenery as almost sacred. She became the voice in Bluffton certain to speak out for what she viewed as the interest of the public and the interest of future generations in public streets, public easements and public accesses to the water.

"We have to look out for these things, or they'll just slip away," she said, always mindful of what such values had meant to her family.

Sara Riley Hooks.

Who Was Michael C. Riley?

Sara Riley Hooks
Born in 1922

*When the small outlying schools in the Bluffton area were consolidated
into a new brick school for blacks on Goethe Road in the 1950s,
it was named the Michael C. Riley School.*

Seven-year-old Sara Riley barely knew her ABCs when she ran out the front
door of her Bluffton home and, with her small brown hands, tenderly scooped
an injured man's intestines back into his abdomen. Split open in a fight, the
man had walked down Bridge Street to ask for directions to Dr. Roland K.
Smith's nearby home. The physician lived just across the street, but Sara felt
he needed immediate emergency medical care and administered it as best she
could. The man recovered from his wounds.

Sara said later that she knew the day she pushed the intestines back into
their natural location that she was "supposed to care for them." As a child,
she doctored birds and cats and when one of her little friends was injured,
she would get some newspapers and a sheet and do the best she could to fix
them up.

"I always had a sixth sense that told me things—like who was pregnant and
who was going to die—before other people knew. And I had the sense, early, to
know that I was supposed to be a nurse."

Sara was born in 1922 to Michael Christopher Riley, a Bluffton native who
had attended Georgia State Industrial College, and Daisy McDowell Riley, a
Charleston native who had gone only as far as seventh grade but who cooked
like a chef and sewed like a seamstress. Daisy had met "Mikey," as Sara's father
was called, when she worked as a stewardess on one of the steamboats that

hauled passengers and freight between Bluffton and Savannah. Daisy and Mikey ran their household of six children with several rules in place. They included the rule that the children must attend Zion Baptist Church on Sunday and the rule that they should eat figs frequently to keep their bowels regular.

And Mikey told his six children day and night, "Your life will be worthless without an education." It was not easy to get an education if you were a black child in Bluffton in the early part of the twentieth century. For blacks at the time, even in population centers, the state officially provided only six months or less of schooling per year and only for six grades. All of the Riley children completed their high school education away from Bluffton—two of them in New York and the other four in Savannah. Eventually, all six made something of themselves. Sara took nurses' training at Waverly Good Samaritan Hospital in Columbia and completed graduate work at the Medical College of Virginia.

PUSHING FOR PUBLIC EDUCATION

Mikey was interested in more children than his own, however. In the 1930s and 1940s, he spent a good deal of his time talking to the Bluffton Board of Trustees about building a school for blacks, about lengthening the school year and about adding grades. He also used his skills as a merchant—and his personal popularity—to raise money to help his cause.

After World War II, when rumors spread that segregation was coming to an end in the South, slowly things began to change. The Beaufort County Board of Education appointed Mikey to the Bluffton Board of Trustees, the governing body for schools south of the Broad River, and simultaneously appointed another black to the governing body for schools north of the Broad River. Many believed at the time that they were the first blacks in the South to serve on school boards.

When the small outlying schools in the Bluffton area were consolidated into a new brick school for blacks on Goethe Road in the 1950s, it was named the Michael C. Riley School. When segregation finally ended in 1970 with the consolidation of the separate black and white schools, the Michael C. Riley School was designated for all elementary students in the Bluffton area, black and white. When a new elementary school was built in the 1990s on Burnt Church Road, it was given the same name.

NURSING IN SOUTH CAROLINA

Beginning in the 1940s, young Sara worked as a nurse in Columbia, Savannah and Dorchester County. In the early days of her career, one white patient announced that she was not going to let "that nigger" give her a shot. When the doctor in charge warned that Sara would give the shot or it would not be given, the patient gave in. After that, Sara said, the woman would always ask for Sara when she came in to see the doctor.

In 1969, when Sara became a home health nurse for the Beaufort County Health Department, her nursing services in the Lowcountry put her into the homes of black, white, rich and poor. She dealt with stroke victims, colostomies, catheters, fevers, wounds—the works. She continued to meet a few challenges because of her race, but she simply took charge of the situations as they arose. Mostly, Sara recalled being treated like a family member by the families she visited: "I was interested in the patients and interested in saving lives. I was not for any foolishness. They respected me for it."

After retiring from public health service in 1979, Sara continued to do private nursing duty and continued to serve her neighbors—as a neighbor. Living on the old Riley home, just off Huger Cove on Bluffton's Bridge Street, she still had the fig tree that served her and her siblings so well. She traded the figs that ripened in the summer for the vegetables her neighbors grew in their gardens—sweet potatoes, Irish potatoes, squash, okra—along with chickens and eggs.

For a long time, besides giving way figs, Sara gave away time and expertise. For many years, Blufftonians called Sara whenever there was a fever or a stomachache in town. She gave advice and often drove folk to the doctor or the dentist, spending her "last five dollars" to buy gasoline for her Cadillac to make the trip. When her gasoline money ran out, she would ride the bicycle to the grocery store down the street.

"I know I'll be all right. I get everything back that I put out. I don't worry."

Ice Cream on Bridge Street

Although Michael C. Riley, his wife and his daughter, Sara, were no-nonsense people about education and about nursing, the Riley family for many years provided a unique source of pleasure to Bluffton-area families. From a little building in their front yard, they ran a grocery and a restaurant, known for its big pans of warm gingerbread, its rice, ribs, pies and cakes. Best of all, with ice imported by steamer from Savannah, Mikey made ice cream every Sunday and served it in cones. The Rileys rented the property across the street and put up swings and benches so people would have something to do on Sunday afternoons when they came to get their ice cream. At the time, it was the only place in southern Beaufort County to buy either ice cream or gingerbread.

In 1953 Sara married William Hooks, a baker from southwest Georgia, and they had one son, Anthony Alexander Dominic Earl John Michael Jose Hooks. Sara gave him seven given names because, she said, she knew at the time she would never have another child. "Tony" graduated from Savannah State

College in biology, then joined the rock group Sly and the Family Stone as a guitarist. For a few years, Tony toured the nation performing while maintaining his personal headquarters at his grandparents' home in Bluffton. Tragically, a gunman killed Tony one night at home.

Sara Riley Hooks continued into her eightieth year to live in the house in which she grew up, just at the edge of Huger Cove, off Bridge Street. She spent the last days of her life in the same place she spent her first days—and would not have had it any other way.

David "Come See" Jones.

BUTTER BEANS
FOR SAVANNAH

David "Come See" Jones
Born in 1927

His toughest adjustment at Penn School was learning to eat at the table with girls.

Butter beans and watermelons made Hilton Head Island's reputation in the 1930s and 1940s, according to David Jones. "In the Savannah City Market, people would be standing round, waiting for my father to get there with the truck of butter beans from Hilton Head. There was a steep ramp that we had to drive up to get in. Movsovitz [the grocery wholesaler] and others would come to bid on the beans. The ladies in their stalls would buy them too. We always tried to let them have some. They shelled them and sold them right there in the market."

A big brick building covering one of Savannah's city squares, the market filled every morning in the heat of summer. The sellers arranged their butter beans, watermelons, corn, peas and okra from farms in the region; their fresh fish and shrimp and still scrambling crabs from local waters; their handmade baskets and quilts; their eggs, chickens and smoked hams. The buyers wandered through, taking in the smells and the sounds, reveling in the joking, bartering and haggling that goes on among traders all over the world.

From the north end of Hilton Head to downtown Savannah was a good day's trip that father Benjamin "Ben" Jones and son David made three or four days a week in spring and early summer. For decades, it had been a boat trip all the way. Soon after the U.S. 17 bridge across Savannah was finished in 1925, Benjamin brought his beans by boat to Buckingham Landing and arranged for a truck to take him and his beans to market from there. In later years, with a thirty-five-foot flat-bottomed boat with a cabin and a Wisconsin air-cooled engine and a big Chevrolet truck of his own, Benjamin began hauling freight for others as well as himself.

David's father was born on Hilton Head and his mother, Mary Jane Hamilton Jones, was born in Bluffton. For several winters, Ben was the chef for the "big house" on Palmetto Bluff. Later, Ben was chef and Mary was kitchen manager for Honey Horn Plantation. Spring and summers, they worked the soil to produce crops for sale in Savannah. Fall was the season of hog killings and cane grindings.

Ben and Mary's first two children died as youngsters. When David was born, his many cousins would call to one another to look at the new baby, "Come see!" David took on the nickname "Come See." A big boy, "Come See" grew up learning to handle an oar the way other children learn to handle a tricycle.

GETTING AN EDUCATION

David was only five when he began walking the several miles from his home on Jarvis Creek to the small one-teacher school at Honey Horn. Later, he had classes at the Church of Christ. After ninth grade, David, in the tradition of many Hilton Head youngsters, became a boarder at the Penn Community School on St. Helena Island, where he worked on the school farm for fifteen cents per hour to pay tuition.

David said his toughest adjustment at Penn was learning to eat at the table with girls. "I was so ashamed to sit at the same table at first that I couldn't eat for about a week. They'd mix us up, a boy and a girl, a boy and a girl. It took me a while to get used to it," he said.

He got used to it and got over it. For all of the fraternizing Penn encouraged during meals, none was allowed without chaperones on weekends or at night. "We were allowed to go to town on Saturday, but we mustn't be seen with girls. On certain Sundays we could sit in the lobby with the girls," he added.

Drafted into the U.S. Navy shortly before graduation, David finished high school through correspondence courses during World War II. A reservist, he was called up again during the Korean Conflict, although he served only thirty-nine days before being discharged as the sole support of his family after his father died.

In 1950 David completed courses in mechanical arts, specializing in auto mechanics, from the North Carolina Agricultural and Technical College. He worked for the U.S. Army Corps of Engineers and in a body shop in Savannah before taking out a loan for $1,800 to open his own garage on Spanish Wells Road. He paid back that loan in monthly installments. Not long afterward, he paid $1,500 cash for his first shrimp boat, a thirty-six-footer named *Birdie*.

A Shrimp Trawler and an Elected Position

The year David "Come See" Jones bought *Birdie*—1967—was the year he was elected to the Hilton Head–Bluffton seat on the Beaufort County Board of Directors (predecessor to the County Council). He was the first black in that seat, the second black on that governing body.

At the same time his public service responsibilities grew, both of his business ventures grew. Shrimp ran strong, and their prices held high in the late 1960s and early 1970s, so he bought two more shrimp boats, *Captain Dave* and *Black Cloud*. He helped organize and became president of the Hilton Head Fishing Cooperative in 1968. Through his work in the co-op, he traveled a great deal and learned the ropes on getting grants from foundations and the government.

In 1970 BASF, the German chemical business, created a storm of controversy by proposing to build a dye factory that would discharge pollutants into the Colleton River. As a demonstration of local fishermen's objections to potential environmental damage, David Jones piloted the *Captain Dave* up the Intracoastal Waterway to Washington, D.C. There they presented the U.S. Secretary of Interior with a petition against the chemical plant, signed by 45,000 South Carolinians—plus a package of local shrimp. BASF backed off.

For a time during the early 1970s, David's life had its hectic moments. He became a partner with Charlie Simmons Sr. in his bus lines in 1970.

"Then that county council job got to be almost full time," he said. "And then I'd work all day at the garage and have to go see about the shrimp boat at night," he said. "I had a good captain, but he couldn't change the oil. I'd have to go down into that engine room, where they had been running all day, and change the oil in the evening. All that, plus the co-op, got to be too much," said the big man, who moved and talked deliberately and quietly.

The first responsibility David shucked was politics. In 1976 he didn't run for office, and Hilton Head Island Republican Gordon Craighead was elected to the seat he had held.

By 1977 the price of fuel was high, shrimp catches were smaller and shrimping equipment had become more expensive, so David got out of shrimp and into fuel sales and delivery. He kept his garage and wrecker businesses and bought buses to expand his transportation service. By then, the bustling growth of the island made it possible for him to live in the place he loved, all the while making a good living.

Recalling that Famous Whistle

In his quiet way, David Jones held closely some personal memories he knew newcomers would never have—among them the sound of the whistle that blew at daybreak summer mornings to summon workers to the Jenkins Island shrimp factory in the 1930s. "I'd be asleep when it blew, but soon, right outside my bedroom window, I'd see the people starting to walk. They walked all the way from this side of Jarvis to Jenkins Island. There was no other way."

David was one of only a few who remembered the mounded piles of butter beans, fresh from their well-tended rows on the north end of Hilton Head Island, ready for sale in the stalls of the Savannah City Market.

In addition, David had another secret memory about his youth on Hilton Head. It made him laugh.

"We were all taught crocheting, knitting and embroidering in school here," he said, grinning. "I don't know if I can still do any of it now, but I sure learned it."

Abraham "Abe" Grant. *Courtesy of Abe Grant.*

EACH TIME TAKE CARE OF ITSELF

Abraham "Abe" Grant
Born in 1937

Soon he found white kids stopping by to talk and buy Pabst Blue Ribbon beer.

When Abraham "Abe" Grant was twelve, under the tutelage of his uncle, he made the best moonshine on Hilton Head Island, he said. "We would tie a bag across the vat to keep the bugs from falling in. We would use the 'low wine,' the last of the batch coming, to cut the strength of the first batch and to sweeten it. Then my uncle would tie it on his horse and carry it all over the island, to Baygall and Squire Pope and Spanish Wells. Everybody knew it was the best."

In the early 1950s, when there were three sawmills on the island, Abe was able to get what was called "slabs," boards cut crooked, to build himself a store. So eager he was to begin his first business enterprise, he overloaded his horse and wagon and had to unload half the lumber and make more trips than he had planned. Then he opened his own business by the side of U.S. 278, a twelve-by-twenty-foot shop selling honey buns and cold drinks. Soon, said Abe, the store became "the special place for everybody to come."

As a young man, Abe spent four years in Florida, first working for his father on a shrimp trawler fishing out of Key West, then for a dairy in Miami. His pay at the dairy increased from "Class C pay to Class A pay," he said, because, "I was never a lazy person. I didn't stand around waiting for somebody to tell me something to do. I always looked for something to do."

When he returned to Hilton Head Island in 1961, he rode around noticing houses being built in the first wave of modern development in Sea Pines,

North Forest Beach and Folly Field, and he got the idea that maybe the island would have enough population soon to support a good business. He added seven feet to his twelve-by-twenty-foot building and soon found white kids stopping by to talk and buy Pabst Blue Ribbon beer. Soon he realized they were looking for something to do, somewhere to go nights and weekends, and he wanted to fulfill their desires.

"I'm going to build you a night club," he told them.

> So in 1964 I opened Abe's Driftwood Lounge. I cut the neon lights on at 8:00 p.m. and got a call from Fred Hack [early developer] at 8:20 p.m. Mr. Hack said neon lights were something they [he and Charles Fraser] didn't want on Hilton Head. I said, "Well, ya'll must have had a meetin' about neon lights, but you didn't invite me." Still, I didn't want trouble. So Mr. Hack said they'd pay me $90 if I'd just cut off the neon lights and leave 'em off.
>
> I cut the lights off and went to Mr. Hack's office next morning to pick up my money. So it turns out Mr. Hack gave me $45 and told me to go to Mr. Fraser to get the other $45. And that's how we solved the neon lights problem.

The Driftwood Lounge did well. As building picked up on the island, Abe's Driftwood Lounge offered not only live music and a party place, but also lunch for construction workers—hot dogs, hamburgers, sandwiches, soup. "We sold them for $2, then $2.50 and so on—not too much for them to afford the lunches but enough for us to make a little," Abe said.

Beginning in 1968 and then for thirty-two years, Abe Grant and family owned and ran Abe's Shrimp House, probably one of the first restaurants in the nation making a name for itself on okra and tomatoes, sausage and rice, shrimp and grits. Abe said he had the "first buffet" on Hilton Head and was the first restaurant he knows of to make shrimp and grits a menu specialty. Until then, shrimp and grits was just something coastal dwellers put together for an easy supper.

Abe's served lunch and dinner; served locals and tourists; served wage earners and professionals; served sweet iced tea, fried whiting, fried shrimp, deviled crabs, collard greens, black-eyed peas, corn on the cob—the staple items of South Carolina Lowcountry menus—for whites and Gullahs alike.

"We were successful," he said, "because we sold good food at a good price and because my whole family worked in it. My wife, Charlie Mae, did the work of three people. My children all came up working in the restaurant. We had Tony and Carolyn and Lillian and Terry and Abe Jr. They learned to do everything, and they did it. They worked hard."

Abe said he usually stayed back in his office during the busiest hours, would come out to talk with the customers only if he had enough time to chat with all of them. "I couldn't pay attention to some and not others," he said.

ABE AND THE CHILDREN

The family's work, which included running a motel as well as the restaurant, came to a halt long enough for the family to attend church together and then go out to eat together on Sundays. "We'd go to a steakhouse or to Morrison's Cafeteria. We'd often be the only black family in the restaurant. People would come over to us and express how they admired how well behaved the children were.

"Well, they were well behaved. In fact, in our home, there would be ashtrays and trinkets sitting around on the tables when they were little and people would come there and wonder how come the children didn't mess up everything. Well, they didn't mess it up because we didn't allow it. They would see how I would look at them and know."

One day Abe went with a friend to the Beaufort County Courthouse and watched thirty-five or forty young blacks and four to five young whites, he said, milling around waiting to face criminal charges pending against them. "That's when I pulled my children all around this [dining] table and talked to my children. I told them, 'I am not going up and down with you. If you are trying [to do what's right], I'll go broke trying to help you.'

"My family knows I will help them. I'll do all I can to help them, but if they are doing nothing, or they are just trying to be slick, I've got no time for them. If you are not trying, I've got nothing to bail you out. And one more thing," he added, "you pay your bills on time. Don't make promises about Monday if you're not going to take care of it on Monday."

With the restaurant and the motel and with the dining-table talks and Sunday at church, Abe and Charlie Mae sent all five children to college. Then in 2000, the children urged their parents to close the restaurant.

> *A restaurant's some turmoil and frustration now, I tell you. You find out one day your best cook or your best server is not coming to work that day. You got spoilage. You go to make sure the restrooms are clean all the time. People would come to the door and ask to use the restroom. I know what they were thinking. We were black people. They would be white people. If the restroom's clean, they would say to themselves, "The kitchen's probably in about the same condition as the restrooms." So every night I made sure those restrooms were as they should be.*

Then the Pinochle

By 2006 Abe's working and worrying days were mostly over. He was trying hard to perfect his pinochle game. His friends gathered around a table in his living room several times a week, laughing, whooping it up, having a good time with pinochle.

In addition, he was serving on the boards of Van Landingham Rotary Club and the Palmetto Electric Trust and as senior deacon at Mount Calvary Baptist Church.

So how could a fellow raised up making moonshine, a fellow who made a living running a lounge and a pool hall, become a fellow in leadership in the church—a Baptist church, no less?

"Well," he said with a smile, "each time take care of itself." By then, Abe had lived through several different "times" on Hilton Head.

Abe's grandmother, Peggy Grant, he remembered with a corncob pipe in her mouth. His "birth mother" was Bell Grant, a woman never much involved in his life. He was raised by his aunt, Beulah Grant Kellerson, and his uncle, Willie Kellerson, on the family's Chaplin area property across William Hilton Parkway from what became Abe's Shrimp House.

Many Kinds of Education

As a child, Abe walked to a two-room school on what is now Mathews Drive, then rode in the back of a truck to a four-room school on what is now Beach City Road. He finished "three months into eighth grade" and went to school no more. However, at the age of six, he learned to plough. At the age of twelve, he learned to make moonshine. At the age of sixteen he went into business for himself. And his enterprises eventually produced the wherewithal to buy a gold Mark V Lincoln Continental, a diamond ring or two and education in top-notch colleges for his children.

All of Abe's life, he compensated for a lack of formal education, he explained, by being an observer, a listener, a person who asks questions, in addition to being a person who works hard. "I experienced some things in Miami," he said, "watched people make ignorant mistakes. I saw a lot of fights, but I didn't stay around to see who won. I learned that some people are all for themselves, not for you. They are spying to see how they can hurt you, get something from you. I never believed in letting people see you handle money. Watch out for people."

A man of street smarts, common sense and a love of letting the good times roll, Abe Grant also was a man of compassion. "Sometimes I don't feel like goin' to the Palmetto Electric Trust board. But I know there are people, old people, out there who don't have food, don't have heat, don't have air, people we need to help. It makes me feel good to help them so I go to those meetings anyway."

What a character, Abe Grant, and what memories he had of the way things were a while back on Hilton Head Island.

You Might Also Enjoy

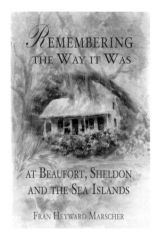

Remembering the Way it Was at
Hilton Head, Bluffton and Daufuskie
Fran Heyward Marscher
978.1.59629.061.7 • 192 pp. • $21.99

Remembering the Way it Was at
Beaufort, Sheldon and the Sea Islands
Fran Heyward Marscher
978.1.59629.136.2 • 128 pp. • $19.99

A Guide to Historic Beaufort,
South Carolina
Alexia Jones Helsley
978.1.59629.045.5 • 144 pp. • $19.99

Sentimental Savannah:
Reflections on a Southern City's Past
Polly Powers Stramm
978.1.59629.140.0 • 160 pp. • $19.99

Visit us at
historypress.net